C000164277

THE ENGLISH
ABBEY
EXPLAINED
Monasteries • Priories

TREVOR YORKE

COUNTRYSIDE BOOKS
NEWBURY BERKSHIRE

First published 2004
© Trevor Yorke 2004

All rights reserved. No reproduction
permitted without the prior permission
of the publisher:

COUNTRYSIDE BOOKS
3 Catherine Road
Newbury, Berkshire

To view our complete range of books,
please visit us at
www.countrysidebooks.co.uk

ISBN 1 85306 854 3

Photographs and illustrations by the author

Produced through MRM Associates Ltd., Reading
Printed by Woolnough Bookbinding Ltd., Irthlingborough

CONTENTS

Introduction

The medieval abbey or priory conjures up distinct images in our mind. Some may think of craggy ruins standing like broken teeth amongst fields or a grid of imposing stone walls laid out upon the bottom of some remote wooded valley. Others might imagine soaring cathedrals, a large number of which were once monasteries, or other great churches that still bear the title Abbey or Priory, revealing their medieval origin. Most, though, will picture hooded monks walking in silence around cloisters or standing with the shaved top of their heads exposed whilst chanting in the church choir.

I have always found it frustrating to match my image of what a medieval abbey would have looked like with the fragmented remains that I can visit today. Some sites have only an information board to explain the ruins, while those with guidebooks often concentrate on character histories rather than the bewildering stonework that I have paid to see. The general publications available on the subject either tend to get bogged down with technical and historic details or are too lightweight, leaving questions unanswered and the features I see unexplained. It was with the intention of plugging the gap between too much information and too little that this series of books was born.

Using my own drawings and diagrams, and photos taken from sites all over the country, *The English Abbey Explained* is an easy-to-understand guide designed to help you identify and understand the features you see when visiting these magnificent monuments. It is broken down into three sections, the first taking you on a historical journey from the origins of these buildings back in the days of the Roman Empire through to their dissolution by Henry VIII. It includes illustrations of their style and period details which may aid in identifying and dating structures, while at the end of each chapter there is a view of 'Exemplar Abbey', an imaginary site designed to give the reader a general idea of what these monasteries may have looked like in each period.

The second section looks at the individual parts of an abbey, from the church and cloisters to the more mundane lavatories and drains, and explains how to recognise them and how they were used. The final part is a quick reference guide, including a time chart to help date buildings, a list of some of the best sites that are open to the public and a glossary explaining some of the more confusing terms that you may come across.

Trevor Yorke

CROXDEN ABBEY, STAFFORDSHIRE

SECTION

I

THE HISTORY

OF

ABBEYS

CHAPTER I

Definitions and Origins

❧ ⚜ ❧

Definitions

Before looking into the history and features of abbeys, it is worth differentiating between the myriad of names that we associate with the subject. A *religious house* is a community of monks or nuns living together, more commonly called a *convent* when applied to the latter (but the term can be used for either sex). In most cases, therefore, a *monastery* is a religious house comprising monks, while a *nunnery* is a convent of nuns (it seems, though, that the word monastery is often applied to all types of religious houses and to both the community of monks and the buildings in which they live).

The important words for the purposes of this book are *abbey*, which is a monastery or nunnery of large size or high status, and *priory*, which is a smaller house, often subordinate to an abbey, although some grew in size and status to become just as important. A *friary* is the home of *friars*, a later group who relied upon begging for their income and spent much of their time preaching in the outside world, as opposed to *monks* and *nuns* who resided almost permanently within their abbey or priory. Between these are *canons*, who are divided into two types: *regular* and *secular*. The former (from the word *regula*, meaning rule) lived like monks by strict monastic rules within their own abbey or priory, but unlike them also preached outside. Secular canons were not connected with monasteries and were usually associated with other religious establishments such as cathedrals and colleges.

The principal member of the community was the *abbot* or *abbess* in an abbey and the *prior* or *prioress* in a priory, the latter often acting as deputies to their superiors at the abbey. Below these on the monastic social ladder were the *obedientiaries*, who were monks put in charge of the various departments of a monastery and typically named after them, like the cellarer, kitchener and infirmarer.

Monasticism is divided into two forms: *eremitic,* where monks live an isolated existence as hermits, and *coenobitic* (derived from the Greek for 'common life'), where the monks spend at least part of their time within a community. Although this book will focus on the latter form and the spectacular abbeys these religious groups built in Britain, eremitical monasticism was not only ever present here, but also appeared alongside the coenobitic form when monasticism first took shape.

The Origins

There have been men and women who have isolated themselves from the outside world to seek a closer union with God since the earliest days of Christianity. A life of denying themselves indulgences

FIG 1.1: *A map of Europe and close up of the British Isles showing the probable route by which monastic ideas spread from Egypt across modern day France and into Britain. This did not happen as one fluid movement but via individuals establishing religious communities at various locations and dates. The flags give approximate dates for the foundations of monasteries.*

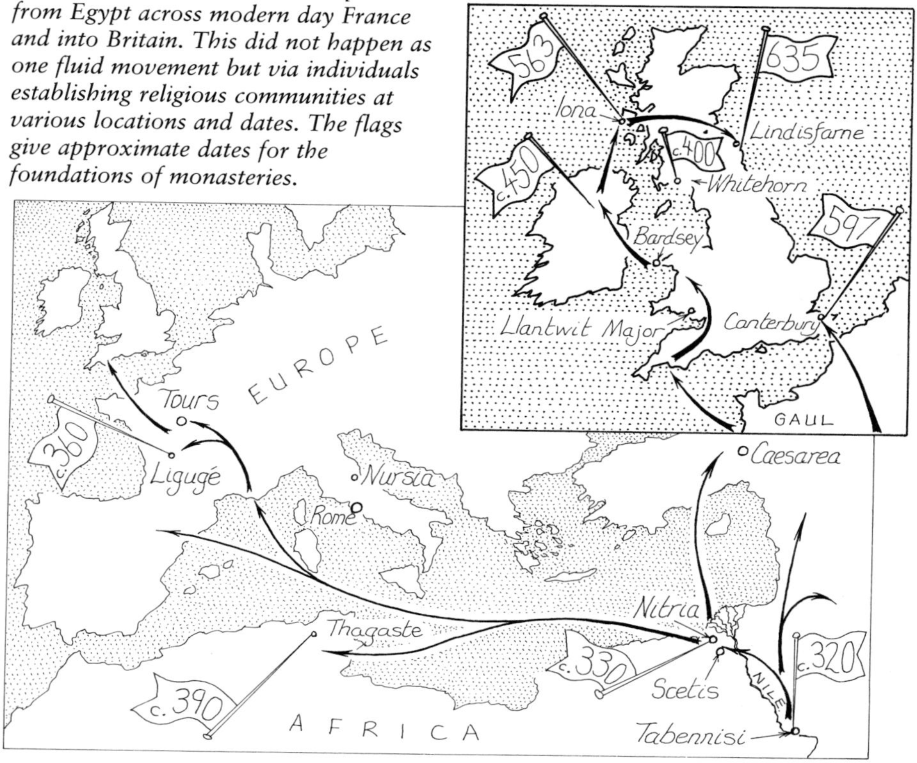

(known as 'asceticism') and spending their days in solitary prayer began to appeal to a growing number of people more than 1,700 years ago. Perhaps inspired by Jesus and his forty days and forty nights spent in the desert, they sought a similar environment, the area along the River Nile, to the north-east of the Sahara (modern day Egypt) proving particularly attractive.

Paul of Thebes was possibly the first of these pioneers, who were later referred to as the 'Desert Fathers', becoming a hermit in his youth and living a solitary life surrounded by the shifting sands until his death around AD 341. St Antony, known as the Father of Monasticism, lived around the same time, spending his final forty years in a hermitage on Mount Kolzim, near the northern tip of the Red Sea. Perhaps more relevant to our story is Pachomius, an ex-soldier who used his military background to form many solitary Christians into disciplined groups of men, with his first community established at Tabennisi in around AD 320.

These early religious houses spread like wildfire, appearing on the outskirts of Egyptian towns and villages and in various isolated locations during the 4th century. They were probably unplanned settlements with wells, an area for cultivation and simple structures containing a single room or cell for the monks, all within a walled enclosure. Mealtimes and services may have been the only occasions on which the members of the community had contact, and it is recorded that even here they did their utmost to ignore one another and preserve their ascetic lifestyle.

This self denial and discipline reached unwelcome extremes as these religious loners sought to out perform each other with increasingly severe punishments. One character, Macarius, chastised himself for killing a solitary mosquito by spending six months naked next to an insect-infested marsh, emerging unrecognisable as his body was swollen and scarred by bites. He also went without cooked food for seven years for no better reason than that he had heard another group of monks did so for the period of Lent. Eventually, this competitiveness, which was itself a sin, was replaced with more reasonable behaviour.

Much of Europe in the 4th century still formed part of the Roman Empire and, with its acceptance of Christianity under the Emperor Constantine from AD 305, the religion was able to spread freely. The Empire was built around trade and there was constant movement of goods and people between countries, making it easy for monastic ideas from Egypt to be transported abroad. Hilary of Poitiers, for instance, had come into contact with monasticism while in exile in the East and on returning to Gaul (modern day France) had along with St Martin (who had already established a monastery in Milan) set up a community at Ligugé. They may have used an existing Roman villa site, a pattern which repeated itself across the old Empire. This illustrates a theme running throughout the history of monasteries – that they were founded by wealthy individuals of high status on estates within their gift.

The First British Monasteries

It is still unclear when the first monasteries were established on the British mainland, although it is unlikely that it was before the departure of the Roman legions in AD 410, which is commonly seen as marking the end of the Empire in Britain. Roman life actually carried on for some time as the remaining Romano British population of some four to five million still dominated the country, but, with the breakdown in the market system, the large cities and towns that it had supported could no longer be maintained. Although already present in Roman Britain, Germanic groups (including Saxons and Angles) began to increase in number, so that by the 6th century the Christian Romano British culture found itself confined to western Britain.

Although it is recorded that monastic sites were founded in the 5th and early 6th century (e.g. Llantwit Major and Bardsey Island in Wales) no site from this Dark Age period has been positively identified. It is most likely that monastic ideas spread from Gaul through the Celtic regions in the west and over to Ireland, as is famously recounted in the story of St Patrick who established a house in Armagh sometime around AD 450. Our story, though, will really begin in the middle and late 6th century, when Christianity returned to the British mainland not just from one source but two.

Celtic and Saxon Monasteries 500-1066

FIG 2.1: BRIXWORTH CHURCH, NORTHAMPTONSHIRE:
A rare surviving church, in part dating from the 8th century.
Ignore the later tower and semicircular stair turret,
it is the main body of the building that was part
of an early monastery. The bottom row of
round arched windows were originally openings into
what are believed to have been individual chapels that stood
up against the sides of the wall.

FIG 2.2: IONA ABBEY, OFF THE ISLE OF MULL: *The structure in the picture is a medieval monastery built on the site of the religious house founded by St Columba in AD 563. The tiny pointed-roof building to the left of the west end of the church (the five windows in a row) is known as St Columba's Shrine and was a chapel, which may date from the 9th century. In front of it are a number of stone crosses, some dating from the 8th century, which probably marked the route for pilgrims to the shrine.*

Brief History

Sometime during AD 563, there came to a small island off the west coast of Mull, an Irish noble who, it is said, was banished by holy men as punishment for slaughtering too many in battle (although it was more likely to have been because he had become too powerful). The man was Columba (later Saint) and his landing place was Iona, where he established a monastery along the lines of a new generation of religious houses he had already founded in Ireland. It was to this monastery that King Oswald of Northumbria, the most dominant power in England at the time, turned for his bishop in AD 635. St Aidan and a group of monks were despatched and settled on Lindisfarne (Holy Island), establishing a community second only to Iona. This Celtic Christianity was spread by others down into the Midlands and the South while, in return, numerous southern nobles travelled north to be baptised.

In AD 597, the year that St Columba passed away, a missionary, despatched by Pope Gregory the Great, landed on the south coast of England. He was St Augustine and with the blessing of the Kentish king he began preaching the Roman form of Christianity at Canterbury, where he also established a monastery. After initial setbacks, the influence of the Roman church spread out of its heartland of Kent and Essex, and headed west and north, where it inevitably came into contact with the Celtic form.

Although fundamentally similar, the two churches nevertheless disagreed on a number of points. One was the tonsure, the haircut of a monk, which under the Roman rules was just shaved on top but in the Celtic form had the front section of the remaining ring of hair removed as well. The principal problem, though, was over the date of Easter, which despite warnings from Rome, the Irish and Northumbrian church continued to calculate from a different point. The Synod of Whitby in AD 664 was arranged to resolve the issue, with the Roman method being ruled correct, although it was still not adopted by some monasteries for more than fifty years.

This mixed birth of the church in Britain left a disordered structure, which Theodore of Tarsus, Archbishop of Canterbury from AD 668–690, set out to reform. He developed ecclesiastical organisation and

FIG 2.3: *An imaginary Celtic monastery set on a windswept island where timber is sparse so even the individual cells, the small houses in which the monks live, are made from stone. The churches, with monumental crosses marking the burial ground, stand in the distance, while a monk tills his garden in the foreground.*

FIG 2.4: WEST STOW SAXON VILLAGE, SUFFOLK: *A reconstructed Saxon house, which, although it is not a monastic cell, does give an indication of how these simple timber structures may have looked.*

restructured the diocese, as well as holding a council at which it was decided that the movement of monks should be restricted so they could not leave their monastery without the abbot's permission. Within this more stable structure monasteries flourished, turning their back on the strict asceticism of the Celtic church and excelling in art, sculpture and learning, and especially illuminated scripts, which gained wide renown in Europe. Unfortunately, their reputation and wealth attracted the attention of unwelcome guests, as in AD 793, longships appeared over the horizon at Lindisfarne. The Vikings had arrived.

Surprise raids of plunder and slaughter devastated the British monasteries, with only a few in the south and west surviving more than a century of incursions by firstly Norwegians and then Danes. It was the latter group that in the 870s came to settle permanently, only to be held at bay by King Alfred of Wessex, who, along with his descendants, eventually gained control of much of England. Under these 10th century Christian rulers, monasteries began to be refounded, especially when Dunstan, the inspirational Abbot of Glastonbury, became Archbishop of Canterbury in AD 960. He played a major part in establishing Benedictine religious houses across the south and east, so that on the eve of the Norman Conquest some 100 years later there were nearly fifty monasteries and nunneries.

Abbeys in this Period

▣ FOUNDATIONS AND SITES

With only fragments of Anglo-Saxon and Celtic monasteries surviving today and little reliable documentary evidence, their appearance in this period requires a certain amount of imagination until further sites like St Paul's Monastery at Jarrow come under the scrutiny of modern archaeology.

Monasteries (referred to at the time as minsters or monastrii) were founded by the rich and influential, and often by the regional royal families. They would grant estates, usually measured in hides (the measure of land required to support a peasant family, which varied from 40–120 acres), which were used to support the new religious house as with little or no land, the monastery would fail. These new estates also gained freedom from certain taxes and tithes, which according to Bede encouraged Saxon nobles to claim to have established a religious house and demand the benefits but never actually accommodate any monks or nuns on the site.

Many early foundations were the first Christian presence in a generally pagan area and the monks were expected to spend some of their time converting the local populace and maintaining services thereafter. When the church authorities laid out their dioceses, some of the more important of these 'missionary' monasteries were used as the seat for the new bishops. He took the status of abbot (although the community was run by the prior), and their church building became his cathedral. Known as cathedral priories, examples from this period include

FIG 2.5: MONKWEARMOUTH CHURCH, COUNTY DURHAM: *The lower parts of this west tower probably date from the 7th century, when the Venerable Bede was beginning his monastic life here at the age of seven. He later spent most of his time at the neighbouring monastery of Jarrow, where he wrote his influential 'Ecclesiastical History of the English Nation', one of the few and more reliable sources of information to glimmer out of these Dark Ages. Both monasteries were abandoned in the wake of Viking raids.*

Canterbury, Winchester and Worcester.

The sites chosen for some of the earliest monasteries, especially Celtic ones, were windswept and desolate, coastal islands and promontories, or marshland, as befitting their strict ascetic lifestyle. As both the coenobitic and eremitic forms of monasticism existed alongside each other at this time, those members who sought complete isolation established separate hermitages away from the main religious house. The remains of some of these can still be found today on a number of tiny, rocky outcrops around Britain's coast.

Some early Anglo-Saxon sites were chosen by those who wished to follow an eremitic lifestyle, yet by their reputation they attracted followers who formed a community and, as a result of the trade and services required by the new monastery, they in turn encouraged urban growth over many years. The towns that eventually enveloped the original monastery would probably have the hermit founder turning in his grave! Later Anglo-Saxon monasteries were less concerned with isolation and do not seem to have had the dispersed hermitages of their Celtic predecessors. They are often located in valley bottoms near to a river or stream, which even at this early date they began using to their advantage.

▦ PLANS AND STRUCTURES

Celtic and early Anglo-Saxon monasteries do not seem to have been laid out to a standardised plan. They are more likely to have appeared as loosely dispersed structures within a round or rectangular enclosure. The church – sometimes there was more than one – and possibly a number of communal buildings were the only structures likely to be of stone. By the 8th century these were probably aligned along an east to west axis and may have been arranged in rows (as has been found at Jarrow). They were surrounded by cells, which were small timber or stone houses for the monks, with an altar or chapel inside and a garden outside. Burial grounds with monumental crosses, workshops, wells and some form of guest accommodation may have also stood within the precinct, which was enclosed by a ditch and bank surmounted by a stone wall or timber palisade (fence).

While the Vikings were beginning their reign of terror upon British monasteries, there emerged in Central Europe an empire, the first of this size since the Romans, which under the rule of Charlemagne and Louis the Pious reached its peak in the early 9th century. At synods held in Aachen during AD 816 and 817 it was decided that the religious houses within this Carolingian empire should adhere to the Rule of St Benedict, an Italian monk of the early 6th century. At the same time they probably adopted some form of standardised plan, which included a single church, with other principal buildings arranged around a square cloister below it. When Dunstan refounded the monastery at Glastonbury in AD 940 and others such as Aethelwold restored communities across the south and east, they built them along the lines of these new European models. Most of these 10th century monasteries lie under later buildings or have been lost within urban areas, although excavation has given glimpses of cloisters and churches, which at this date were smaller versions of the medieval layouts.

The Monks and the Orders

Although monks and nuns are often perceived as remarkably self disciplined, there have been periods of dissent. While the early Celtic monasteries were

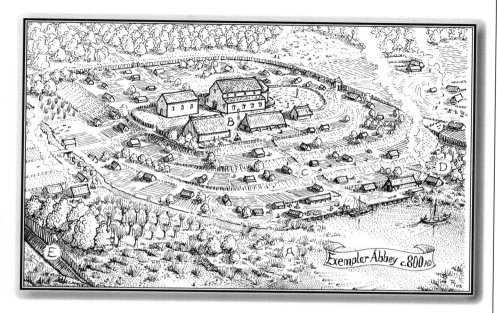

FIG 2.6: EXEMPLAR ABBEY CIRCA AD 800: *On a shallow promontory above the junction (A) of a stream to the left and the main river to the right, monks have cleared the site for their monastery. The principal buildings of churches and communal halls stand on the highest point (B) with the monks' individual cells, no more than small huts with a plot of land, scattered on the terraces below (C). Down by the river in the bottom right corner are workshops alongside a small quay (D) that was used for bringing in some of the building materials, while the whole site is surrounded by a ditch and fence, best seen in the bottom left (E). This successful establishment has probably heard of a distant Viking threat but is unprepared for the devastating century it is about to enter, leading to its violent and dramatic demise.*

renowned for their adherence to a strict ascetic lifestyle, some Welsh and English monasteries gained a reputation for greed and excessive eating and drinking. One monk is recorded as leaving his religious house in disgust at the drunkenness of his abbot, a man who later became a saint!

In the pre-Viking period, the monks and nuns seem to have followed no standardised rule but lived by one produced locally, possibly a combination inspired partly by their founder and partly by that written down by St Benedict of Nursia. This latter Benedictine rule, reformed on the Continent in the 9th century, was adopted by Dunstan and his followers for their refounded Anglo-Saxon monasteries. After a Great Council meeting held in AD 973 it was decided that the monks and nuns who lived in the forty or so religious houses should all be Benedictine.

Still Out There

FIG 2.7: ST EDWARD'S CHURCH, LEEK, STAFFORDSHIRE: *(Right) The remains of a Saxon cross, probably dating from the 11th century. Examples from the 7th–11th centuries can be found in various parish churchyards and monastic sites across the country and could have been used as a preaching place, burial cross, or marker for pilgrims.*

FIG 2.8: *(Left) This section of masonry from a Saxon circular tower has distinctive bands of stone laid at 45° in what is called a herringbone pattern, a style typical of the 11th century.*

FIG 2.9: BREEDON ON THE HILL, LEICESTERSHIRE: *The Anglo-Saxon monastery which once stood upon this notable hill is long since gone, yet in the later parish church, which stands precariously above a quarry cliff face, fragments of remarkable carvings of saints, monsters and geometric patterns from this early religious house can still be viewed.*

FIG 2.10: RIPON CATHEDRAL, NORTH YORKSHIRE: *Buried below the body of the medieval building, accessed down an inconsequential staircase, is a simple, dimly lit Saxon crypt. This rare survivor probably dates from the original monastic church erected on this site by St Wilfred in the 8th century and was used to house holy relics, with doorways in and out for the flow of pilgrims.*

FIG 2.11: DEERHURST, GLOUCESTERSHIRE: *Saxon windows were generally crowned by either semicircular arches or triangular shaped heads, as in the example dating from the 10th century. At the time this church was a Benedictine priory.*

FIG 2.12: BRIXWORTH CHURCH, NORTHAMPTONSHIRE: *Some Saxon windows were simply cut from a single stone, as in this example. Originally all these windows were open, with shutters or oiled skins to keep the draughts out; the glass in this picture is much later.*

FIG 2.13: BRIXWORTH CHURCH, NORTHAMPTONSHIRE: *The triumphal arch leading from the chancel into the curved apse beyond has a semicircular head composed of Roman bricks, reused by Saxon masons from a local ruin. Under the apse were stored holy relics, which could be viewed by pilgrims from the ambulatory that ran around the outside and was accessed from doorways in the chancel – note the blocked one in the bottom right of the wall.*

FIG 2.14: ST JOHN'S CROSS, IONA: *A replica of an 8th century high cross, in front of which pilgrims would pray en route to St Columba's Shrine, which is the small building directly behind it.*

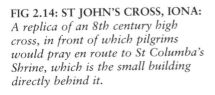

CHAPTER 3

Norman Abbeys
1066-1200

FIG 3.1: ST ALBANS CATHEDRAL, HERTFORDSHIRE:
When the first Norman abbot, Paul de Caen, was installed after the Conquest, he set about rebuilding the church with his master mason from Normandy to direct the Saxon workmen. With little local stone available, they reused the bricks that lay around from the ruined Roman town of Verulamium. Much of this work survives in this view: the north transept on the left, the tower in the centre and the nave on the right.

Brief History

The arrival of William the Conqueror and his success at the Battle of Hastings led initially to an intense round of castle building as the French barons, who had flocked to his banner with the promise of rich pickings, endeavoured to secure their new English estates. These lands had been granted to them by the king as he replaced the Saxon hierarchy with Norman nobles, including abbots from leading religious houses like Jumièges and Bec in Normandy. Here there had been vigorous monastic reforms during the 11th century and the existing English abbeys were inevitably influenced by these spiritual and cultural changes.

Although a number of abbeys were erected in the years following 1066, most notably Battle Abbey, founded by the new king on the site of the conflict near Hastings, William's barons were initially more concerned with the monasteries back in Normandy. The major investment required to rebuild and found new abbeys was only forthcoming when the Normans felt more sure of their new possessions, towards the end of the 11th century. Whereas the Saxons tended to venerate old buildings and erected separate new structures when additional space was required, the Normans simply flattened the old English abbeys and started from scratch with new, massive, elongated, stone churches designed to fill the local populace with awe. These were not necessarily of better quality, though, as Anglo-Saxons were renowned across Europe for their sculpture, metalwork and illuminated manuscripts, and were regarded by many as artistically and culturally superior to the Normans, whose descent from their pagan Viking ancestors spanned only six generations!

As monasticism continued to grow, the new abbeys and priories began to reflect changes on the Continent and they were no longer exclusively of the Benedictine Order. The abbey at Cluny in France had grown in influence across Europe since its 10th century foundation, becoming ever more willing to despatch its monks to kings to advise on reforms, establish new foundations, act as ecclesiastical advisers and even as abbots or bishops. With a weak papacy they were allowed to develop independently, so by the 12th century a new version of the Benedictine Order had evolved. Known as the Cluniac Order (the Anglicised names of most new orders were derived from that of the abbey in which they were conceived), the first foundation in England was at Lewes in 1078.

Another group to arrive from the Continent before 1100 were the canons regular, who, unlike Benedictine and Cluniac monks, went out into surrounding communities to preach. The earliest canons followed the word of St Augustine and their first site was at Colchester in around 1093.

FIG 3.2: ST BOTOLPH'S PRIORY, COLCHESTER, ESSEX: *Although this Augustinian priory was the first in England, founded around 1095, this dramatic west front of the church dates from the late 12th century, with the characteristic set of diminishing arches around the doorways and bands of blind arcading above. As at St Albans, this was built with reused Roman bricks, which were already some eight to nine hundred years old at the time. Although it may look dull today, at the time it was usual for the exterior to be rendered or whitewashed over, with details and statues picked out in bright colours.*

FIG 3.3: FURNESS ABBEY, CUMBRIA: *This strip of decorative tiles was from the original Savignac abbey, which was founded in 1127 after the first site at Tulketh near Preston, Lancashire had proved unsuitable. Quite a few religious houses moved sites in the 12th century, particularly Cistercian. When the Cistercians, who absorbed the Savignacs in 1147, rebuilt the church, they reincorporated this strip in one of the south transept chapels.*

The church had battled for much of the 11th century to separate itself from lay society, so that its bishops and abbots were not granted their offices by the king but were independent representatives of God through St Peter and the Pope. It was thought that even the lowly priest should be seen as an individual above the level of ordinary men, so marriage was banned and celibacy encouraged. The reformed monasteries, influenced by Cluny, further enhanced these ideals, perceiving themselves as Noah's Arks in a sea of violence and disorder, sanctuaries where gifted and devout individuals could lead a separate life from the turbulent society around them. In France towards the end of the 11th century, though, a number of monks broke away from these so-called reformers, disillusioned that they were increasingly immersing themselves in lay society through their advisory roles and displaying the trappings of wealth, with elaborate church buildings, decoration and ceremony. This was a long way from monasticism's roots with the Desert Fathers in 4th century Egypt and it was their example that inspired these individuals to form new houses which grew into the new orders of the 12th century.

The most notable of these new orders was that of the Cistercians, founded in 1098 at Citeaux in Burgundy (West France), who arrived on these shores in 1128 at Waverley in Surrey. Another early group were the Savignacs, whose most notable house was Furness Abbey in Cumbria until they were absorbed by the Cistercians in 1148. The Gilbertines were the only English order and were founded by a Lincolnshire landowner, St Gilbert of Sempringham, in 1131. Premonstratensian canons (from Prémontré in France), who modelled themselves on the Cistercians, arrived a little later, in 1143, at Newsham in Humberside.

This was the boom time for monastic foundations, so that the fifty or so monasteries in existence at the Conquest had increased to about five or six hundred by 1200. For all the popularity of the new orders, though, Benedictine houses still dominated in number and tended to be the wealthiest.

The Abbey in this Period

▣ FOUNDATIONS AND SITES

In this early medieval period, it became fashionable that after a gruesome battle or barbaric murder the remorseful noble could redeem his sin in the face of God by donating land to an existing religious house or by establishing an abbey or priory. This, it was assumed, would protect the soul of the benefactor and his family, and was one of the principal driving forces behind the frenetic bout of monastic building in the 12th century.

In the first decades after the Norman Conquest, though, the nobility tended to grant their new English estates to abbeys back in France rather than risk founding new houses in an unstable and unfriendly country. The fortunate French abbey might despatch a couple of monks to manage the farm, land and church from a manor house complex, so that no monastery as such was built, while others founded small priories which operated

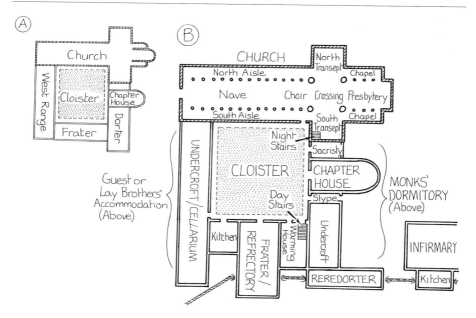

FIG 3.4: *Two plans of cloisters, showing in (A) a layout typical of a small priory and some of the early Norman abbeys and in (B) a larger establishment, which may have been a later expansion of (A). Note the round ended chapels, presbytery and chapter house in (A) and the short square end to the church, as was the fashion in the later 12th century in (B).*

along similar lines. The famous abbey at Bec in Normandy was granted such land, and this is still recorded in the English place-names of Weedon Bec in Northamptonshire and Tooting Bec in London. Because they transferred wealth to France, with little spiritual return, however, these establishments quickly became resented and in the anti-French fervour of the Hundred Years' War (1337–1453), they were labelled 'alien cells and foundations' and were eventually abolished.

Once the Normans were established in power, there was a boom in monastic foundations, fuelled by the kings and great nobles of the age. They would grant a site for a new abbey or priory, along with a number of estates, the produce and income from which would support the new foundation. The more land that was close to the religious house, the wealthier the monastery would be destined to become, as it would be easier to manage and control. It didn't necessarily matter whether the land was suitable, as the well-educated and practical monks were gifted at land clearance and agricultural improvement, especially when it came to drainage.

The type of site chosen for the patron's foundation would to some extent depend upon which order was invited to run it. Many Cluniac houses were situated near to the major castles of their royal or baronial founders. The Augustinian canons attracted large congregations to hear their preaching and their houses were usually located near population centres in towns and cities, although some were founded on ancient monastic sites. The new orders of the early and mid 12th century sought sites to replicate the barren sands endured by the Desert Fathers, but in our wet climate they had to make do with wasteland, marsh or forest in remote corners of the country. The Cistercians are well known for finding such locations and are recorded as bravely hacking out an existence from these inhospitable places, especially in the north of England. The truth was often less dramatic, though, as by the 12th century in most parts of the country there was someone eking out a living, however meagre. The Cistercians are known to have picked locations where a hermitage already existed or to have moved whole villages from their prospective abbey or priory site just to maintain their isolation.

A factor which was appreciated by nearly all orders by this time was the need to position monasteries near to a water supply, usually beside a river. Although flooding was a problem and a number of abbeys and priories were re-sited for this reason, the flow of water was crucial for cleansing purposes. Rivers were diverted in man-made channels, running under kitchens and flushing out toilets before returning to their original course (see fig 9.10). It was also quite common for the whole length of river adjacent to the new monastery to be run into a new channel along one side of the valley bottom to provide room for buildings or fields (see fig 10.5).

◼ PLANS AND STRUCTURES

As religious houses sought to provide an isolated sanctuary, cut off from the outside world, the arrangement of the principal buildings in a square enclosing a cloister, which had appeared in the later Saxon monasteries, still proved the ideal layout. Although the scale of the plan grew and the increasing number of orders made minor alterations to it to suit their individual requirements, this enclosed arrangement was to last throughout the Middle Ages.

The basic layout placed the most important building in the complex, the

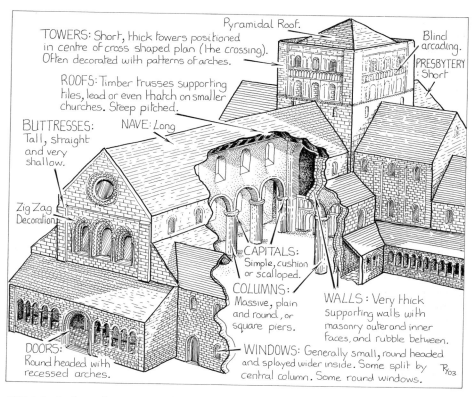

TOWERS: Short, thick towers positioned in centre of cross shaped plan (the crossing). Often decorated with patterns of arches.

Pyramidal Roof.

Blind arcading.

PRESBYTERY: Short

ROOFS: Timber trusses supporting tiles, lead or even thatch on smaller churches. Steep pitched.

BUTTRESSES: Tall, straight and very shallow.

NAVE: Long

Zig Zag Decoration.

CAPITALS: Simple, cushion or scalloped.

COLUMNS: Massive, plain and round, or square piers.

WALLS: Very thick supporting walls with masonry outer and inner faces, and rubble between.

DOORS: Round headed with recessed arches.

WINDOWS: Generally small, round headed and splayed wider inside. Some split by central column. Some round windows.

R/03

FIG 3.5: *A view of a Norman abbey church as it would have appeared in the 12th century, with a cut-out exposing the interior and labels highlighting the style of its various features.*

church, to the north of the cloister in order to protect the open area from the cold winter winds, although if there were obstructions, like the River Wye at Tintern Abbey, then the plan was reversed and it stood to the south. The church itself formed a cruciform shape on the ground, with the long body aligned on an east-west axis. The wings of the cross plan (the transepts) and the section at the east end containing the presbytery tend to be short and stubby on Norman churches, although they were often lengthened at a later date.

(Look at the walls inside and out for a change in style to pointed arches to indicate where a section has been added on or rebuilt.) The east end was often rounded with small circular rooms built along either side or spread around its perimeter, each one containing a separate chapel or tombs, until by the later 12th century a square end had become the fashion.

The style of Norman churches is Romanesque, a term coined by Victorians, meaning simply 'in a Roman style'. This meant they used the round arch, which,

FIG 3.6: FURNESS ABBEY, CUMBRIA: *This stunning set of five Norman round arches are quite late for this style, dating from the early 13th century. The three nearest ones mark the entrance to the chapter house with a book cupboard either side of its entrance, the last two arches opened onto a parlour and a slype, a narrow passage which led out to where the monks had redirected the watercourse to flow under the reredorter (toilets) and kitchen.*

because it relies on being a perfect semi-circle for its strength, cannot be widened or stretched vertically if a larger building is required. With these limitations, the Normans simply built thick in order to build big. Immense walls with a rubble core between the inner and outer stone skins, stocky circular columns and square piers for support, and round arched openings stacked in bands upon each other to gain height all helped form their massive structures, which were intended to leave rebellious Saxons awestruck.

The roof of the main body of the church was usually of lighter timber construction. The technical knowledge required to build elaborate stone vaulted ceilings over these wide spaces was beyond most Normans, though they achieved simple versions along the narrower aisles to the side. The majority of windows around the monastery would have been open, with shutters, oiled cloth or animal skin used to keep out the chill. Important windows, especially those in the church, could have been fitted with stained glass, imported from France or Germany (we could only make limited clear glass in the early Middle Ages), and held within an armature or network of metal bars (the stone tracery bars which divide most church windows today developed in the 13th century).

Benedictine and Cluniac houses received elaborate decoration, with intersecting arches carved in stone forming blind arcades on walls, and zigzag or chevron patterns radiating around windows and doors. By the late 12th century, deeply recessed doorways surrounded by decorated, graduating stone arches were popular, a fashion taken from Henry II's newly conquered lands in southern France. These features were not just confined to the church, with the chapter house on the east side of the cloister often blessed with a stunning triple doorway, sculptured wall recesses and a stone vaulted ceiling.

In contrast to this glorious and imposing architecture, the new orders of the 12th century – especially the Cistercians – built simply, with plain interiors devoid of lavish decoration and

Fig 3.7: BUILDWAS ABBEY, SHROPSHIRE: *This monastery, like that at Furness, was founded by the Savignac Order, only to be absorbed by the Cistercians in 1147. This photo shows the nave of the church and (typical) of early Cistercian construction, it is simple and plain, the only decoration being small scallops around the capitals above the stocky round columns. Also note that the arches have a slight point, a style imported by this French order, although the row of clerestory windows above are still small and round headed, typical of Norman churches.*

with towers of only moderate height. They did, however, import with them the idea of a pointed arch, although at this early date these were little more than a kink at the top of a semicircle. This more adaptable form was to change the whole structure and decoration of stone buildings in the following centuries.

The Monks and the Orders

Whereas the Saxon monks followed a lifestyle laid down by St Benedict, with a few local variations, the post-Conquest monks were guided by new and invigorated interpretations of the rule and different ways of organising their monasteries, most of which originated in the great abbeys of France.

The Benedictines were never really an order but more of a community of relatively independent monasteries. They wore black capes and cowls over their cassocks and were thus known as the Black Monks, only being referred to as Benedictines later in the Middle Ages. They were renowned for their learning, teaching, writing and art and flourished in the reigns of William I and his sons, with their largest abbeys, such as Glastonbury, becoming some of the most important and wealthiest in this country.

Cluniac foundations were all daughter houses of the mother church at Cluny and were therefore only priories under the control of the abbot in France. This centralisation, along with understaffing and lack of finance right from the start, meant that few ever developed into efficient monasteries. Despite this their order was both generous and glorious. They did much to support pilgrims and the poor, yet lavishly decorated their churches and spent much time involved with worship, liturgy and ceremonies.

Augustinian or Austin canons were also priests, so although they followed a rule they could also go outside of their precinct to preach. They proved popular with nobles, who could employ them to take services in churches for which they were responsible without having to find a permanent incumbent, a fact which might partly explain their rapid growth, with 140 new foundations in the 12th century. They were also notable for founding hospitals – two survivors being St Bartholomew's and St Thomas' in London. Their black cloaks gained them the name of the Black Canons.

With the new orders of the 12th century came changes in the way the monasteries were organised and the monks lived. In their remote and austere surroundings, Cistercian monks led a life based around prayer and manual labour. Despite this, much of their work was actually done by the conversi, or lay brothers. They differed from the quire monks (the fully literate monks who spent their time at prayer in the church quire, or choir) by having shortened periods of prayer and a better diet to aid their time out in the fields and workshops (meat, eggs, cheese and butter were restricted for quire monks). Conversi were never taught to read or write and lived in separate wings to prevent any ambition or ideas of progress!

The Cistercian order also rejected the incomes from churches and gifts of settled lands, endowments which financed most other institutions at the time. Instead, they established a network of monastic farms known as granges, often on some form of waste or upland area, where they most notably bred sheep. Control over these self-sufficient monasteries was administered through annual chapter meetings at Cîteaux which each abbot had to attend. The dramatic increase in the number of new foundations in the 1130s and 1140s made this difficult, so the foundation of new Cistercian monasteries

FIG 3.8: IONA NUNNERY, OFF THE ISLE OF MULL: *A view of the church dating from around 1200 at this house of Augustinian nuns, one of the few nunneries with substantial remains today.*

was forbidden from 1152 (although their numbers still increased). Their austerity even ran to the banning of warm underclothes and furs, leaving just their habits of undyed wool – which resulted in them being known as White Monks.

Premonstratensian canons had a similar interpretation of the Augustinian rule as the Cistercians did of the Benedictine. They, too, chose remote sites, emphasised manual labour, used conversi and had annual meetings at the mother church at Prémontré. In their role as

priests, though, they still held services at other churches, including those belonging to canonesses of the same order and Cistercian nuns.

Although double houses containing both monks and nuns were not unusual in the Saxon period, they were rare after the Conquest. The Gilbertines, the only home-grown monastic order, had them, with Augustinian canons and Benedictine nuns living in the same complex but never permitted to see each other. They might share the same church and hear the same

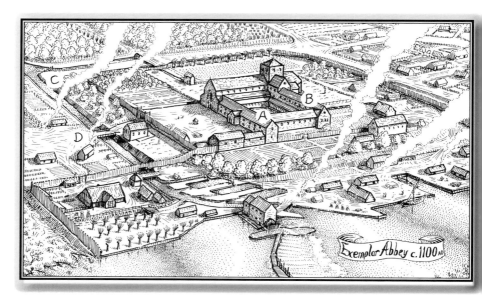

FIG 3.9: EXEMPLAR ABBEY c1100: *Shortly after our last visit, 300 years earlier, the monastery was devastated by Viking raiders and largely abandoned. In the revitalised days of the 11th century it has been refounded and a new set of monastic buildings erected around a cloister on the site of the original church (A), but as was often the case more accurately aligned in an east-west direction. Accommodation for the monks is now in communal dormitories (B), so the surrounding land within the precinct can be dedicated to vegetable gardens, orchards, farm buildings, fishponds, workshops and a new mill by the river. The stream which flowed down the left side in the last view has been re-channelled with a diversion taken off in the top left corner (C) and into the monastic complex to serve the kitchens and flush out the drains. Alongside the new channel a few buildings with their own chapel by the abbey entrance have appeared (D) although the old settlement on the east side is also expanding.*

service but a division built within prevented eye contact.

Knights Templars were fighting monks, established out of the Crusades, who combined their military duties with adherence to the Cistercian way of life. They had a network of preceptories centred upon the London Temple but their great wealth led to their downfall in 1312 when the Pope suppressed the order under pressure from Philip IV of France, who had half an eye on

their money. The word 'temple' in a place-name may indicate that it was one of their estates or the site of a preceptory. The Knights Hospitallers, another military order who focused upon hospital work, took over many of the Templars' houses when they were dissolved.

There were far fewer nuns in medieval England than monks (at best only one in five), which is the reverse of the situation today. They mainly came from the upper classes and could be unmarried daughters, widows of nobles, relatives of senior ecclesiastical figures, or rejected wives. Their houses were usually small, and few ever grew to any note. They followed the rule in much the same way as their counterpart monks. Being female they were unable to take services so a monk of the same order would have officiated – or in wealthier houses a separate chaplain may have been provided (this was not a problem in double houses). There were also limitations with administering their estates, so a male steward may have resided within the precinct to fulfil this role.

Still Out There

PERIOD DETAILS: ROMANESQUE/ NORMAN STYLE

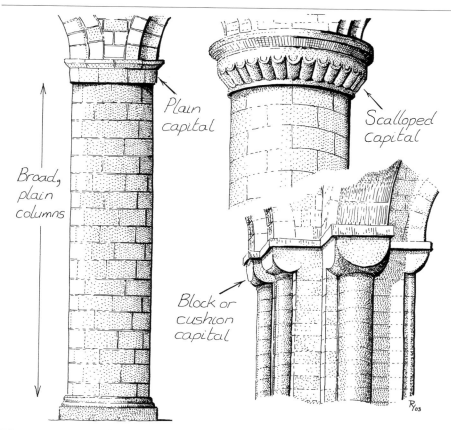

Plain capital

Scalloped Capital

Broad, plain columns

Block or cushion capital

FIG 3.10: *Norman columns. Earlier ones tend to be round and stocky with plain capitals, although square and polygonal shapes were used (sometimes alternating with round ones). Later types had more decoration, scalloped and cushion capitals being popular.*

FIG 3.11: MUCH WENLOCK PRIORY, SHROPSHIRE: *A section of wall decoration in the chapter house of this Cluniac monastery, with intersecting arches (blind arcading), which were popular in the 12th century. Originally these would have been whitewashed over and then decorated in vibrant colours.*

FIG 3.12: ST ALBANS CATHEDRAL, HERTFORDSHIRE: *A round headed opening with two internal arches supported on a column from the tower of the monastic church (see fig 3.1), a popular design for many Norman windows. Note the reused Roman brick in its construction.*

FIG 3.13: MALMESBURY ABBEY, WILTSHIRE: *This spectacular late 12th century porch entrance is the best example in the country of the fashionable receding bands of highly decorated arches, a style imported following Henry II's conquests in southern France.*

FIG 3.14: GLOUCESTER CATHEDRAL, GLOUCESTERSHIRE: *A Norman triforium opening featuring columns with scalloped capitals and chevron or zigzag decoration.*

**FIG 3.15:
TEWKESBURY
ABBEY,
GLOUCESTERSHIRE:**
*Two views of this
well-preserved
Norman abbey
church. The top one
is of the tower,
typically stocky with
rows of blind
arcades, round
arches and zigzag
patterns. Note at the
bottom the
triangular marks on
the walls, which is
where the original
Norman roof stood.
Roofs at this date
were steeply pitched
and could be covered
with tiles, oak
shingles and even
thatch. The second
view is of the west
front with the
impressive concentric
arches, which along
with the tower date
from the mid 12th
century.*

CHAPTER 4

The Abbey at its Peak
1200-1350

◄─ ═◊═ ─►

FIG 4.1: CROXDEN ABBEY, STAFFORDSHIRE:
This rather late Cistercian foundation of 1178 features buildings completed in the early 13th century in the new Gothic Style. Gone are the semicircular forms; now the arches are pointed, with the two lancet windows on the tall ruins of the south transept (in the background), typical of this Early English architecture. The diagonal marks forming a triangle over these are from the roofline of the dorter range, which butted up to this wall.

FIG 4.2: WHITBY ABBEY, NORTH YORKSHIRE: *This dramatic hilltop ruin is of the chancel (east end) of the Benedictine church erected early in the 13th century, with the contemporary rows of tall lancet windows. It had been refounded in 1078 as a priory, only rising in status to an abbey sometime in the following thirty years.*

Brief History

The 13th century marks a high point in medieval history. England was relatively stable and not embroiled in expensive foreign wars. Trade, especially in wool, was profitable and, thanks in part to improvements made by monastic groups, agricultural yields were increasing. Yet even this was proving insufficient to support a growing population, which from a figure of around two million at the time of the Conquest had more than doubled by 1300.

The boom in monastic foundations and new religious orders was drawing to a close. The church legislated in the 1220s that there should be no new orders, yet at the time the differences between the old ones, the Benedictines and the Cluniacs, and the later reformed orders, such as the Cistercians and the Premonstratensians, were disappearing. For all their attempts at isolation the Cistercians and others had, like the Cluniacs before them, become wealthy, influential and more involved in secular society, resulting in a relaxation of their austere rule. With rich returns from agriculture, new and old monasteries alike could afford to erect impressive new churches and cloister buildings to accommodate greater numbers of monks and lay brothers or to further enhance their glorification of God. Many of our finest ruins today date principally from the late 12th to the early 14th century.

At this point there was another bid, the last during the Middle Ages, to return to an austere and strict form of monasticism, from which the new orders of the 12th century had been tempted away. This was made by the friars, who, like the canons in the century before, were preachers and divided into orders, in this case: the Franciscans, Dominicans, Carmelites and Augustinians (not to be confused with the Augustinian canons). The difference was that the friars were mendicants – that is, they relied on begging and lived without possessions. As they did not need a noble to grant them an endowment before they could start preaching, these evangelical groups spread rapidly across Europe,

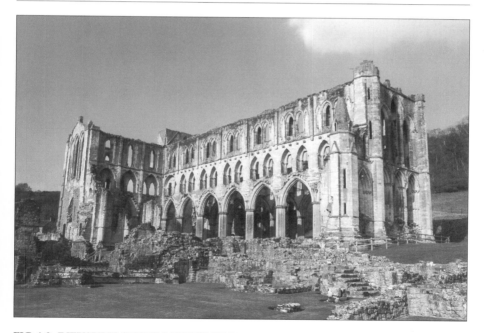

FIG 4.3: RIEVAULX ABBEY, NORTH YORKSHIRE: *It was common for the previously short east ends of monastic churches to be rebuilt in the prosperous 13th century. Here the spectacular presbytery dating from the 1220s stands against the transepts, although the west end beyond has long since gone.*

FIG 4.4: MATTERSEY PRIORY, NOTTINGHAMSHIRE: *This Gilbertine house founded in 1185 was typical of many late 12th and early 13th century small-scale foundations, and its limited endowment was stretched to the limit when most of the site was destroyed by fire in 1279. The picture shows the ruins of the humble refectory, which today stand at the end of a muddy track in the flat open landscape near the Lincolnshire border.*

arriving in England in the 1220s and becoming a presence in most of the major centres of population by the end of the century.

All levels of society relied fundamentally upon the success or failure of agriculture, either directly from goods produced or through the rents charged for others to farm their land. There were only a few, small-scale industries for other sources of revenue should the harvest fail. Monasteries, for instance, were efficient at utilising all aspects of their estates, including lead mining, iron smelting and stone quarrying, from which they made

money and produced raw materials for their buildings. By the late 13th century, however, it was apparent that too much woodland had been grubbed up in order to plant crops (assarting) and the Cistercians were among the first to regulate the cutting and replanting of trees to reverse this trend. With virtually no new land available for corn, the growing population overstretched the system and it would only take one major catastrophe for it to break down. Unfortunately there were two.

A change in the climate and the resulting failure of harvests from 1315–17 resulted in famine across the country and left a weakened population, more susceptible to disease. Any reduction in output would mean less income for the monasteries, so one way of assuring a regular sum of money was to lease out farmland for a fixed rent, so that someone else took the risk. This had started to prove popular among landowners in the 13th century, but even the Cistercians, whose whole structure revolved around direct farming of their granges, had by 1325 begun doing the same. This downturn, though, was nothing compared to the horrors that lay around the corner. In the summer of 1348,

ships arriving at ports along the Dorset coast unwittingly imported rats infested with fleas, the carriers of the bubonic and pneumonic plagues that had decimated Asia and Europe. The Black Death had arrived.

The Abbey in this Period

▣ FOUNDATIONS AND SITES

By the early 1200s, the explosion of monastic foundations was petering out. During the 12th century it had been the kings and nobility who had endowed new houses but now it was minor barons and

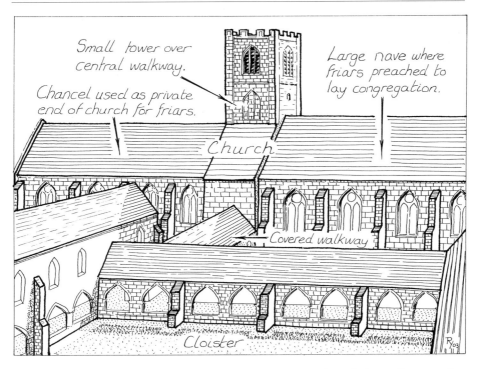

FIG 4.5: *A view primarily showing a distinctive friary church with the walkway under the small tower dividing the nave and chancel and the cloister running below the building to the left foreground.*

local lords who followed the fashion of advertising their status by establishing a monastery. However, their restricted funds tended to result in small priories that were often short-lived, with a handful of monks and on an unsuitable site. By the mid 13th century even this type of foundation had become rare.

The majority of new foundations in this period were those of the friars. They rapidly established themselves in urban locations to be close to the large congregations they wanted to preach to, so that by 1300 the Dominicans, Franciscans, Augustinians and Carmelites were present in all of the main towns and cities. As by this period most of these urban areas had been well developed, there was little room left, so the friars had to make do with small and awkward locations, often on poor land.

▣ PLANS AND STRUCTURES

The somewhat limited sites granted to the friars tended to shape the plan of the buildings they either constructed or took possession of. Some were never more than a modest collection of timber structures, which may have sufficed, as they generally lived in small groups and spent much of their time out and about fulfilling their missionary role. Larger friaries had a layout based around a cloister but its alley was often pushed under the enclosing buildings to save room. Their churches had large naves, sometimes with wide aisles down the sides, in which they preached to a congregation, and a separate, thinner choir at the other end. Between the two was a passage that probably led from a main entrance into the cloister, sometimes with a tower above it.

The plans of the existing monasteries still centred upon the cloister, and although many of the buildings around it were enlarged in the 13th century, the secluded square of land in the middle usually remained the same. One common solution to the problem of creating a larger refectory was to turn the building at an angle of 90° so it could be extended in length, thus preserving the original cloister (see fig 3.4). Another fashion from the late 13th century was to build the chapter house to a polygonal plan, usually with a central column sprouting ribs at the top to form the ceiling and support the roof (see fig 8.6).

In this period of feverish rebuilding, it was the new Gothic style, based around the steeply pointed arch, as had developed in France in the 12th century, which shaped the style of structure and decoration. As most religious orders had regular contact with their founding abbeys on the other side of the Channel it was inevitable that the latest architectural fashions there should easily pass over to our shores. Although trickier to build, the pointed arch was more flexible and graceful. Over here we tended to use it in a style that became known as 'Early English'.

Steeply pointed, arched doors and tall, thin windows known as lancets, set in pairs or groups of three and five, were popular. Small columns attached to a central core or banded together to form a large solid pier (composite columns) can still be seen from this date and had more decorative capitals than before, with simple naturalistic or foliage patterns on top (see fig 4.11). Now masonry ceilings supported by curving stone ribs (rib vaulting) could span larger spaces and were found covering the central body of the church and hiding the wooden trusses that held the steeply pitched roof above it. Although the roofs rarely survive in ruined abbeys, the corbels (supporting brackets) and bottoms of some of the ribs can still be seen high up on interior walls (see fig 4.13).

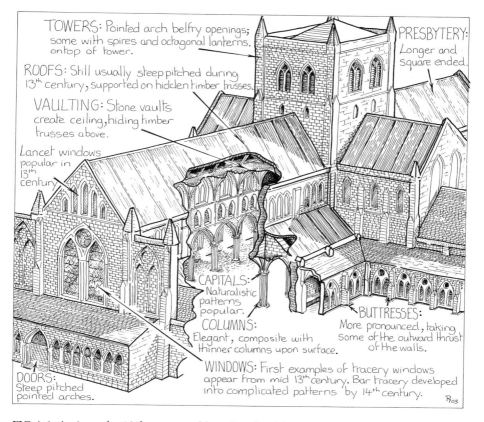

TOWERS: Pointed arch belfry openings; some with spires and octagonal lanterns. on top of tower.

ROOFS: Still usually steep pitched during 13th century, supported on hidden timber trusses.

VAULTING: Stone vaults create ceiling, hiding timber trusses above.

Lancet windows popular in 13th century

PRESBYTERY: Longer and square ended.

CAPITALS: Naturalistic patterns popular.

COLUMNS: Elegant, composite with thinner columns upon surface.

BUTTRESSES: More pronounced, taking some of the outward thrust of the walls.

WINDOWS: First examples of tracery windows appear from mid 13th century. Bar tracery developed into complicated patterns by 14th century.

DOORS: Steep pitched pointed arches.

Pr03

FIG 4.6: *A view of a 13th century abbey church with a cut out exposing the interior and labels highlighting the style of its various features.*

During the 13th century, larger windows were designed, at first with simple openings appearing to be cut out of a flat piece of stone – known as plate tracery – then from the mid 13th century the more familiar bar tracery became common, using bands of stone to make more elaborate shapes. This developed into dramatic sinuous (curvilinear) patterns marking the Decorated style, which dominated ecclesiastical architecture in the early 14th century. These could make

stunning additions to existing churches and principal abbey buildings and often replaced earlier simple openings (hence be cautious in dating a building purely from the style of windows, as they may be later insertions).

Norman builders relied on the sheer mass of the walls to counteract the force of the pitched roof as it tried to push the sides of the structure outwards. As windows became larger and more numerous, the now weaker walls required more support and the previously thin buttresses became more pronounced in the 13th century, although in churches much of their mass is hidden within the aisles which run up the sides.

The Monks and the Orders

Although strictly speaking not monks – as they were outwardly mobile rather than confined to cloisters – the impoverished friars, full of enthusiasm for preaching and teaching, and willing to work as well as beg for their living, became very popular with lay society in the 13th century. Their numbers boomed with new recruits and benefactors, much to the concern of the existing religious orders and secular priests whose roles and incomes they threatened. Friars also made valuable contributions to the establishment of universities, and pupils included the philosopher and scientist Roger Bacon, who himself became a Franciscan friar.

The Dominicans, also known as the Black Friars after the colour of their habit, were the first to arrive in the country, around 1221 at Oxford, and were closely associated with the fledgling universities. The Franciscans, or Grey Friars, spread rapidly across the country in the following decade, taking in recruits from the lower classes (whereas most monks and nuns were of noble lineage). The Carmelites, or White Friars, were initially hermits (their name derived from Mount Carmel in Palestine, where they were first established), with sites in remote parts of the country, but after reform in the mid 13th century they, too, founded communities in the towns and cities. The Augustinian or Austin friars were the final major group to arrive, formed by the Pope in 1256 from groups of hermits. They also had sites in both the town and countryside. It is not the remains of friaries that are

most notable on a map today, but the names of the different orders – for instance, Greyfriars and Blackfriars – can still be found in a number of our towns and cities, indicating where they once resided.

The dramatic success of these mendicant orders was in contrast to the decline in benefactions for the established monasteries, with the abandonment of their founding values and increasing wealth tarnishing their haloes in the eyes of patrons. Royalty and nobles began to look elsewhere for sacred groups best equipped to guide their soul through the afterlife.

Although there were variations between the different orders and, of course, the seasons, the monastic day was always divided up by a strict timetable of church services, the first three of which were often before daybreak. You can imagine half-conscious monks filing down the night

FIG 4.7: *The first picture (opposite) shows early plate tracery from the mid 12th century at Much Wenlock Priory. The second view (left) from the Valle Crucis Abbey shows later bar tracery, which, composed from masonry ribs, has formed curvilinear patterns typical of the first half of the 14th century.*

stairs from their dormitory into the church for matins at 2 am. Between the services, time was set aside for study, meditation, work, rest and chapter, which was a meeting held every morning where matters concerning the abbey's business and the confessions and punishment of monks could take place (a chapter from the rule of that order would also be read, hence the name of the meeting and the room in which it took place, the chapter house). Communal mealtimes in the refectory were accompanied by further sermons and a limited repast, perhaps no more than bread and vegetables, although in this period of relaxing rules, fish, cheese and wines were also consumed.

For a few of the quire monks, known as obedientiaries, there were additional responsibilities. The precentor was in charge of the church services, the sacristan of the robes and holy vessels, the cellarer

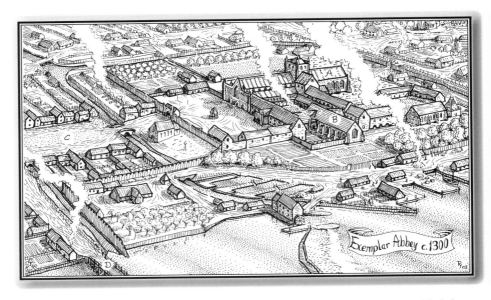

FIG 4.8: EXEMPLAR ABBEY c1300: *Increasing wealth and numbers have enabled the monks to rebuild the east end of the church (A) and erect a new refectory at right angles to the cloister (B) so as not to limit it length. The abbey was also responsible for laying out a new market place and houses (C), a planned development popular with landowners in the late 12th and 13th centuries, designed principally to bring in extra income from rents and fees. The success of this has also resulted in a new bridge across the river (D) as this small settlement evolves into a fledgling town. The future looks bright for all involved!*

was responsible for food and drink, the kitchener looked after the cooking and the fraterer the serving of the dishes. The remainder of the cloister came under the chamberlain, while outside its confines the hospitaller provided a welcome for guests and pilgrims, the infirmarer looked after the sick and old, and the almoner distributed alms to the poor. All of these were under the prior, who himself was responsible to the abbot, selected by the monks themselves as a father figure to the community. He originally would spend most of his time working and sleeping alongside his fellow brothers, but as the

wealth and importance of the monastery increased, the abbot might find himself a lord of many estates, mingling with royalty and nobles, and even sitting in Parliament. Abbots increasingly expected to live like their secular contemporaries, which put pressures upon the rules and layout of the abbey, just one of the changes which would shape monasteries in the final centuries.

Still Out There

▣ PERIOD DETAILS: GOTHIC, EARLY ENGLISH AND DECORATED STYLES

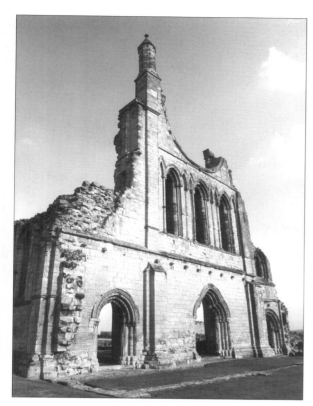

FIG 4.9: BYLAND ABBEY, NORTH YORKSHIRE: *This fragmented west front dating from the early 13th century stands up like a broken tooth from the surrounding fields. It shows the pointed arches, three tall lancets and the base of a huge round window, as was popular at the time.*

FIG 4.10: JERVAULX ABBEY, NORTH YORKSHIRE: *A row of narrow, pointed lancet windows typical of those found on 13th century buildings within the precinct, with these fine examples dating from 1200.*

Dog tooth

Keel moulding

Naturalistic foliage patterns

'Stiff' Leaf

Early English

Decorated

Early English

Decorated

FIG 4.11: *Columns and capitals from this period.*

FIG 4.12: SHAP ABBEY, CUMBRIA: *The base of a composite column. The petal shaped groove running around the base of the shafts was a common detail in the 13th century.*

FIG 4.13: ROCHE ABBEY, SOUTH YORKSHIRE: *Rib vaulted ceilings rarely survive in ruined abbeys but as in this early example from the late 12th century the impost which supports a few remaining sections of the ribs above can often be found high up on the walls to show where they once stood. Note the stiff foliage decoration on the capitals at the bottom of the picture.*

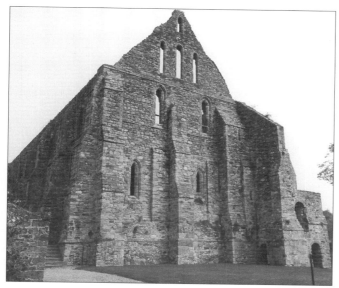

FIG 4.14: BATTLE ABBEY, EAST SUSSEX: *The 13th century monks' dormitory has typically narrow pointed windows and more pronounced buttresses supporting the walls compared with the shallow types used on Norman buildings.*

FIG 4.15: HAILES ABBEY, GLOUCESTERSHIRE: *A 13th century doorway leading from the cloister into the church. This abbey was a late foundation (1246) and twenty-five years later was presented with a phial of holy blood, a relic which attracted pilgrims and additional income.*

FIG 4.16: GLOUCESTER CATHEDRAL, GLOUCESTER: *An example of 13th century rib vaulting. Although it rarely survives in ruined abbeys today, the lower sections that spring off the wall can often be found (see fig 4.13).*

FIG 4.17: ST ALBANS CATHEDRAL, HERTFORDSHIRE: *A section of the nave, showing the earlier Norman work with its plain and massive construction on the right and a later Gothic pointed arch and finer composite columns on the left.*

CHAPTER 5

The Late Medieval Abbey
1350-1536

FIG 5.1: FOUNTAINS ABBEY, NORTH YORKSHIRE:
Despite the original restraint of Cistercian architecture, imposing alterations seemed to have been permissible by the late 15th century. Abbot Darnton reroofed the Chapel of Nine Altars (itself a dramatic addition of the 13th century) and inserted the large window in the middle of it (centre of the picture). More notable is the huge 170 ft tower built onto the north transept by his successor, Abbot Marmaduke Huby, in the early 16th century. This work demonstrates that these men were obviously confident of a prosperous future for their abbey.

FIG 5.2: THORNTON ABBEY, HUMBERSIDE: *The most flamboyant and largest of monastic gatehouses, rebuilt in its present form after 1382 when a licence to crenellate was received, probably in reaction to local unrest in the previous year of the Peasants' Revolt. Behind the façade of very early brick with stone dressing was refined accommodation for the abbot and his guests. The projecting walls of arches either side of the entrance path form a barbican, added in the 16th century.*

Brief History

The Black Death, the devastating bubonic and pneumonic plague, ravaged the country from 1348–49, killing approximately one in three people. Even abbots and monks locked away in their private cloisters were not immune, although more crucially the lay brethren who worked their estates were badly affected. In the aftermath of the pestilence and its periodic reappearances, these conversi disappeared from the scene, as most monasteries chose to lease out their lands and make do with what were now reduced rents as their income.

With a smaller population to work the land, those peasants that were left began to expect improved conditions and opportunities, ideas the ruling classes ruthlessly suppressed, igniting discontent which most famously erupted in the Peasants' Revolt of 1381. By this time, surprisingly, the once revered monks had themselves become a target for these rioters. Their displays of wealth, their tendency to stray from their original rules, and a general feeling that they were out of touch with lay society began to shatter the monastic image. From the 13th century there are records of attacks on monks and abbeys, their reaction to which was to erect new stone walls around the precincts and substantial gatehouses across their entrances. In the medieval world military and religious matters were never expected to be mixed (except in specific cases, such as the Knights Templars) so these inappropriate defensive structures with battlements and arrow loops must have further distanced the monks from the lay population.

While the country was devastated by plague and protest, England had become embroiled in war with the old enemy, France, in a series of battles from 1337–1453, collectively known as the Hundred Years' War. This gave the kings the opportunity to finally close a lingering anomaly from the Norman period, the 'alien cells and foundations', which were now seen as draining English wealth back to French abbeys and permitting enemy spies to reside within the country. The larger houses gained independence or

became dependencies of English abbeys, while much of their estates was redistributed to the new favourite religious foundations of royalty and nobility, one of which was the Carthusians.

The Carthusian Order, named after their original monastery in south-east France, La Grande Chartreuse, where they were founded back in the 11th century, had already established two English monasteries, both in Somerset, at Witham in 1180 and Hinton in the 1220s. Their austere, solitary lifestyle did not prove popular at the time and it was more than a hundred years before they found favour in the troubled 14th century. Seven more of their distinctive charterhouses were built after 1340.

The Carthusians' dedication to their

FIG 5.3: HAUGHMOND ABBEY, SHROPSHIRE: *In this period abbots increasingly built themselves impressive new halls and private chambers, often in separate buildings, like this example with a massive south window and two doors below leading to the service rooms.*

strict way of life was in contrast to the established orders, which began to soften their rules now that they were out of the religious limelight. Abbots and priors built themselves private lodgings, halls and chambers. Monks, who also sought better conditions, might have soft bedding and a wider diet, while greater provision had to be made for an increasing number of guests. This was a period of renewed pilgrimage, and monasteries were expected to cater for passing travellers and visitors to their holy relics and tombs (lucrative possessions for hard-pressed abbeys). Extra pressure for room was also applied from corrodians, people who had paid the monastery a sum of money in return for a guaranteed income and lodgings in their old age (a form of pension). Although this was an effective way of raising cash quickly, it could drain the religious house financially at a later date and cause disruption to the monks. To make matters worse, the king could also force an abbey to accommodate a retired servant or soldier for no recompense. Some space was found within the abbey by converting vacant rooms when the number of monks was reduced or by building new guest houses. Others solved the problem by establishing inns outside the precinct and a number of these ancient hostelries still stand today near the sites of long since vanished abbeys and priories.

The decline in population and the lack of agricultural manpower hindered the country's economy for at least a century. The old feudal order broke down, and a new breed of opportunist men, merchants and yeoman farmers became influential in society. The abbeys themselves had to look for every opportunity to enhance their dwindling finances and one popular method was the appropriation of parish churches. It was common for an abbey's original endowment to contain grants of a limited share of income and control from parish churches belonging to their patron. However, from the early 1300s, monks often sought to gain complete authority over these finances. Despite further enhancing their unpopularity, this time with the bishops, the practice carried on right up to the 16th century. By this period, the financial standing of many abbeys had taken a turn for the better and, although the number of monks was still well below pre Black Death figures, some abbots decided to display their new wealth with rebuilding work in the latest Perpendicular style. Most notable are the dramatic church towers they erected, despite in the Cistercians' case their breaching their original rule on discreet architecture. These structures demonstrate the abbots' confidence that their houses were now over the worst and looking forward to a bright future. Few then could have imagined the sudden and devastating events just around the corner.

The Abbey in this Period

◙ FOUNDATIONS AND SITES

Now that monks had lost the ear of God in the eyes of lay society, the wealthy looked to others for the safe passage of their souls through purgatory. Since 1274 the church had established methods of intercession to relieve the suffering in this temporary state between our world and the next, the most popular being payment for the chanting of mass in memory of the donor. Known as chantries, permanent memorials could range from colleges, similar in layout to a monastery and manned by secular clergy whose principal role was to pray for their founder, to smaller chapels, most commonly built onto a side of a parish church and containing the patron's tomb.

As a result of this redistribution of

FIG 5.4: ST MARY'S COLLEGIATE CHURCH, WARWICK: *The aristocracy in this period often attempted to guarantee the safe passage of their soul through purgatory by founding collegiate churches and building chantry chapels, as in this stunning example for the Beauchamp family, the Earls of Warwick.*

endowments, there was little left for the established abbeys; some small houses closed while others kept going by living off their existing possessions, although the reduced income from these and a general drop in new recruits hampered their ambitions. Not all were bereft of benefactors. Nunneries, which relied on the dowries granted to them by incoming aristocratic novices, survived as they were willing to welcome applicants from the wealthy new merchant class, while many friaries, especially Franciscan ones, never lost the respect of townsfolk and continued to receive new members and possessions.

In a time when the spectre of death hung over king and peasant alike, the stronger a prayer the more chance that the soul would be saved, and it was believed that

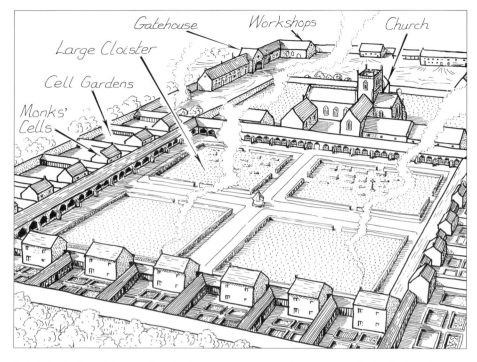

FIG 5.5: *A plan of how a Carthusian monastery may have originally looked with its individual cells and gardens set around a large cloister.*

the more austere the religious group the more potent their blessing would be. It was for this reason that the Carthusians, with their severe and isolated lifestyle, became virtually the only monastic group to found new houses in this period. Their charterhouses were endowed by the wealthiest in the kingdom and established in remote locations in the countryside. Another group to find royal favour were the reformed and strictly uncompromising Observant friars, this time after the first Tudor, Henry VII, ascended the throne in 1485. They had a number of sites, usually founded near royal palaces, but their impact was limited, as their patron's son

was soon to bring the curtain down on all monastic life.

⬡ PLANS AND STRUCTURES

The Carthusians differed from other major orders not only in living an eremitic lifestyle (like hermits) but also in having a unique layout to house them. Their monasteries were centred around a much larger than usual cloister, with individual houses or cells set in their own walled gardens laid out around it. As the monks spent most of their day praying, working and eating within their private enclave there was less demand for communal buildings and these do not dominate the site as in other monasteries.

Despite financial restrictions, existing religious houses still managed to erect new structures during this generally depressed period. Stone walls with battlements were raised around the abbey precinct, lightweight defences designed to hold out rebellious locals or Scottish and Welsh raiders. Impressive gatehouses emblazoned with statues and coats of arms of benefactors were built over the entrances, their upper floors also providing accommodation, chapels and even prison cells (the abbot was often lord of the manor and responsible for its court). As the abbots sought to keep up with their noble contemporaries, they separated themselves from the monks' dormitories and either converted the often vacant east

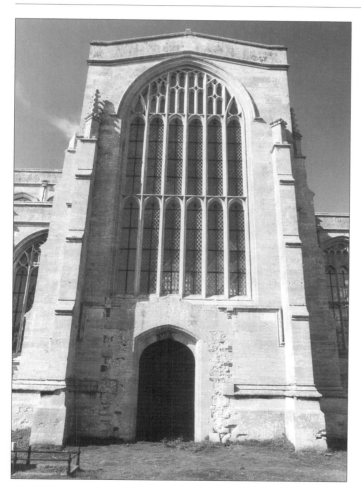

FIG 5.6: HOLY TRINITY COLLEGIATE CHURCH, TATTERSHALL, LINCOLNSHIRE: *This excellent example of a Perpendicular window with the multiple vertical bars (mullions) running the full height of the opening and a transom across the middle is typical of the 15th century. The pronounced stepped buttresses clasping the corners and the flat arch of the doorway below are also notable period details.*

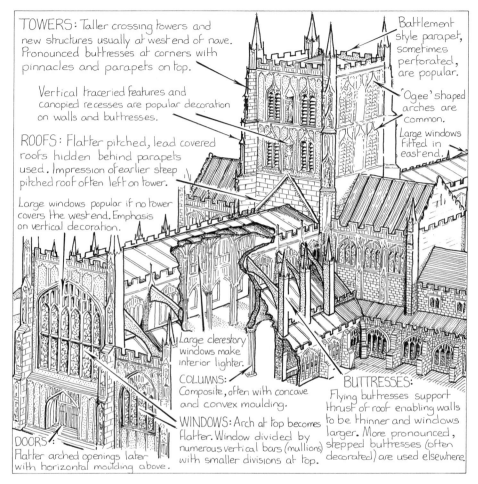

TOWERS: Taller crossing towers and new structures usually at west end of nave. Pronounced buttresses at corners with pinnacles and parapets on top.

Vertical traceried features and canopied recesses are popular decoration on walls and buttresses.

ROOFS: Flatter pitched, lead covered roofs hidden behind parapets used. Impression of earlier steep pitched roof often left on tower.

Large windows popular if no tower covers the west end. Emphasis on vertical decoration.

Battlement style parapet, sometimes perforated, are popular.

'Ogee' shaped arches are common.

Large windows fitted in east end.

Large clerestory windows make interior lighter.

COLUMNS: Composite, often with concave and convex moulding.

WINDOWS: Arch at top becomes flatter. Window divided by numerous vertical bars (mullions) with smaller divisions at top.

DOORS: Flatter arched openings later with horizontal moulding above.

BUTTRESSES: Flying buttresses support thrust of roof enabling walls to be thinner and windows larger. More pronounced, stepped buttresses (often decorated) are used elsewhere.

FIG 5.7: *A view of a 15th century abbey church with a cut-out exposing the interior and labels highlighting the style of its various features.*

or west side of the cloister into their private apartments or built a new hall, chambers and service buildings to the south or east of the infirmary.

The monks also, who were mostly sons of the nobility, had by this time been brought up in fairly luxurious accom-

modation at home and so expected the same standards when they entered monastic life. Consequently, dormitories began to be divided up and separate fireplaces provided. These new recruits were also more likely to have gone to university and, as better educated monks,

FIG 5.8: MOUNT GRACE PRIORY, NORTH YORKSHIRE: *(Top) An external view of a reconstructed Carthusian monk's cell with his garden and covered walkway on the rear wall leading to his latrine. The interior photo (bottom) with glazed and shuttered windows and a fireplace shows how high the standard of accommodation was by the early 16th century compared with the timber hovels which most peasants still resided in.*

required a separate library rather than just a wall cupboard to hold the books they used. Accommodation was also expected for the growing number of visitors and pensioners, resulting in further conversion of dormant rooms and buildings or new structures, usually on the public west side of the cloister.

There was little expenditure on great architectural works until later in the 15th century, when improved conditions encouraged a number of ambitious abbots to erect bold new church towers. Usually sited at the west end of the nave, they

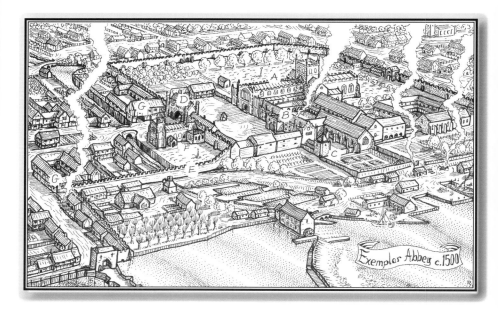

FIG 5.9: EXEMPLAR ABBEY c1500: *The financial constraints of the preceding two hundred years have seen little dramatic change within the precinct, although the church has a new flat roof built behind a battlemented parapet (A). One of the abbots has taken the opportunity while numbers of monks have declined to convert the east range into his private apartments (B), with his own kitchen and garden to the south (C), while unrest from locals encouraged him to build a new gatehouse (D) and precinct wall (E). The town that the monks in part founded back in the 12th century has grown around its successful market, and the church beside the gatehouse has been rebuilt (F) and a number of inns (G) have appeared to provide lodgings for abbey visitors. Despite the economic gloom of the previous centuries the monks looking out of their abbey might feel that prosperity was just around the corner, yet only a few decades later the better informed abbot may have been preparing himself for an impending storm.*

could be huge structures up to 150 ft tall with projecting buttresses running up the corners and pinnacles and battlements around the top. These exemplified the Perpendicular style, which dominated any new buildings in this late medieval period (the word is derived from the Latin for plumb line and the structure and decoration of this style emphasised the vertical). With the use of deep or flying buttresses and lighter lead-covered roofs, the side walls of churches could be made thinner and have a greater area of glass. Huge new windows with flatter arched tops and filled with numerous vertical stone bars lightened the interiors (see fig 5.6) while the stone vaulting above developed into elaborate patterns climaxing in the fan vaulted ceiling (see fig 5.16). The ogee arch, comprising a concave then convex line, was popular and used in windows, belfry openings and on the small canopied recesses that were a common decorative tool.

The Monks and the Orders

Like the hermits of early monasticism, Carthusian monks spent most of their time in their cell. In the 15th and early 16th century they could expect to have living rooms, a study, an oratory and a workshop so that they could carry out their essential prayer and trade in solitude, while hatches in the walls enabled servants to deliver meals without disturbing them. Outside, a tall wall enclosed a private garden, with a secluded cloister, a toilet and a drinking water tap completing their seemingly self-sufficient enclave. They were, however, still required at certain communal services and chapter meetings throughout the day.

Despite their austere eremitic lifestyle, Carthusian monks could expect stone houses with fireplaces, glazed windows and a fireplace, well above the standard of accommodation for the majority of the population at the time. Monks in the existing orders expected even more, with relaxation in their diet permitting meat and fish, paid servants to carry out tasks so they would have more study time, the granting of pocket money and even time for holidays! These were not chances for them to hoist up their cassocks at the seaside, but were periods when the rules of silence and diet were relaxed, usually after their periodic bloodletting. This essential part of medieval medicine was carried out typically from four to ten times a year, depending on the order and individual. Afterwards the drained monk could convalesce in the infirmary or in some cases at a separate house or grange owned by the abbey.

It was in this period especially that many of the rumours concerning the behaviour of abbots and monks arose. There are records of excessive drinking, internal feuds resulting in acts of violence, monks leading raiding parties and enjoying hunting too much. Some had affairs with local women and even fathered children, while nuns were found to be sleeping with young girls and wearing silks. Many abused their office, making personal financial gains from their community. These lax standards and arrogant behaviour lowered the image of the religious orders still further in the eyes of the lay population, which would add justification to the actions of the newly divorced King of England in 1536 – the Dissolution of the Monasteries.

Still Out There

▣ PERIOD DETAILS: PERPENDICULAR

FIG 5.10: RIEVAULX ABBEY, NORTH YORKSHIRE: *A piscina (in which holy vessels were washed) with an ogee arch above. This style of arch with 'S' shaped sides was very popular in the 14th and 15th centuries.*

**FIG 5.11:
CROYLAND
ABBEY,
CROWLAND,
LINCOLNSHIRE:**
*At a number of
monasteries the
local parishioners
had use of part of
the abbey church,
in this case the
north aisle, onto
which they built
their own tower
(to the left in this
view) in the late
15th century. The
right hand side is
the west end of
the monks' nave,
with sculptured
figures still
standing within
their canopied
niches, again
probably dating
from the 15th
century. At most
ruined abbeys
these figures
would have been
destroyed in the
years of religious
turmoil from the
1530s to the
1650s.*

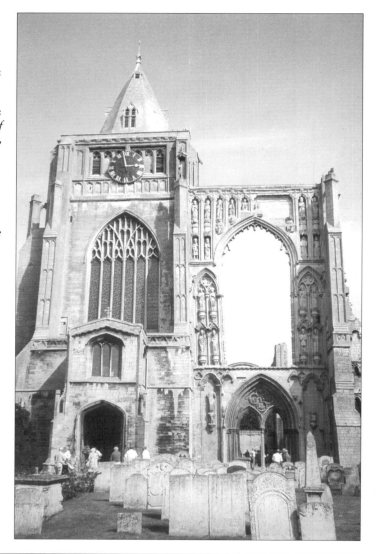

FIG 5.12: SHAP ABBEY, CUMBRIA: *(Opposite) The remains of the early 16th century
west tower (note the stepped buttresses clasping the corners) dominates the remains of
this abbey of Premonstratensian canons, who like the Cistercian Order on which they
had modelled themselves had breached their original rules in erecting such a
prominent structure.*

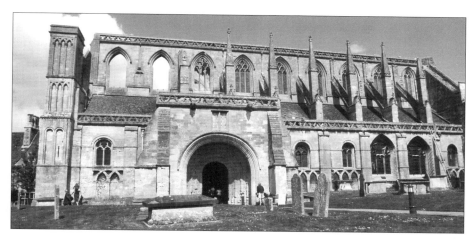

FIG 5.13: MALMESBURY ABBEY, WILTSHIRE: *(Above) This Norman church (in fact it is only the nave that is in this picture) with its spectacular entrance (see fig 3.13) had a new flat roof fitted in the mid 14th century so that the wall of the clerestory below could be raised and the top row of pointed arched windows inserted to give more light inside. The flying buttresses on the right side supported the extra thrust the flatter roof created and the pinnacles on top were not just decorative but added extra weight to hold it all in place. Originally on the far right there was a tower with a spire (which were popular additions in this period) of a combined height of 431 ft, most of which fell down in a storm in 1500, and beyond it the east end and transepts. Only the nave survived the dissolution, when it was granted to the parish as their nearby church was in a parlous state.*

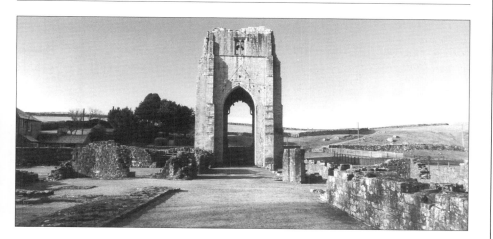

FIG 5.14: MOUNT GRACE PRIORY, NORTH YORKSHIRE: *A doorway to a cell, with a flat arch and ribbed moulding above it, which were becoming popular in the 15th century. The square hole on the right was the hatch where the lay servants left the monk's meals so they would not come in contact with each other, while the shields on the top corners of the door had either carved or painted coats of arms of the noble who originally endowed the cell.*

FIG 5.15: MALMESBURY ABBEY, WILTSHIRE: *An interior view of the stone ribbed ceiling fitted at the time of the work in fig 5.13. The pattern is known as Lierne vaulting and differs from the earlier rib vault in fig 4.16 in having extra short ribs between the main ones which are purely decorative. These developed into more elaborate patterns in the 15th century.*

FIG 5.16: TEWKESBURY ABBEY, GLOS: *A richly decorated porch on the south side of the church with Perpendicular features such as canopied recesses above the door (bottom), and a small segment of fan vaulting on the ceiling above.*

FIG 5.17: CHESTER CATHEDRAL, CHESHIRE: *The refectory of this former monastery still survives with a hammerbeam roof, an ingenious development in carpentry which permitted large spaces to be spanned without the need for inconvenient aisles.*

CHAPTER 6

The Dissolution of the Monasteries and the Fate of the Abbeys 1536 onwards

FIG 6.1: CHESTER CATHEDRAL, CHESHIRE:
This Benedictine abbey, founded in 1093, became a cathedral in 1541 after its dissolution, with the abbot becoming the new dean. Today there is still much to see from the medieval abbey including cloisters, chapter house, gatehouse, and the refectory – which is appropriately the cathedral restaurant!

FIG 6.2: EASBY ABBEY, NORTH YORKSHIRE: *A view showing the refectory to the right, with its pointed windows of c1300, and the dormitory to the left, unusually to the west of the cloister. Shortly after it had been dissolved in 1536 this Premonstratensian abbey was repossessed by monks during the Pilgrimage of Grace before the rebels were dispersed and in the following year savagely dealt with by Henry VIII.*

The Dissolution of the Monasteries

If only Henry VIII had approached the Pope for divorce from his first wife Catherine of Aragon a few years earlier, then the devastation of the medieval monasteries may never have taken place. Unfortunately, in 1527 the Holy Roman Emperor, Charles V, had sacked Rome and made Pope Clement VII a virtual prisoner, so when Cardinal Wolsey began negotiations that year to secure a divorce he met with failure, for as luck would have it Charles was Catherine's nephew and he would not let her be cast aside.

Henry's desperation for a male heir, intensified by passion for his new love, Anne Boleyn, forced him to break with Rome and make himself Supreme Head of the Church of England, enabling his new archbishop, Cranmer, to declare his marriage to Catherine null and void. One immediate problem was the presence in the country of religious foundations that owed allegiance to the Pope, namely the monasteries, and their removal was seen as crucial to maintain his fledgling Anglican church. The fact that it would enable him to transfer their property and wealth into the treasury's beleaguered coffers and use grants of land to secure the allegiance of nobles was probably just as important.

In 1535 surveys of monastic resources and moral standards were carried out and, armed with this information, Thomas Cromwell, the king's secretary, convinced Parliament to pass the Suppression Act in the following year. This legislation called for the closing of the smallest religious houses with an annual income of less than £200, in which it was claimed lax observance of rules was most likely to occur. Despite commissioning preachers to prepare the lay population by convincing them that monks were idle and hypocritical, there was surprising resistance to the Act, especially in the North, culminating in the most serious threat to Henry's reign, the Pilgrimage of Grace. In late 1536 a Yorkshireman, Robert Aske, unified the rebels, including members of monastic communities, who opposed many aspects of Henry's policies and were ignited into action by the Suppression Act. The 40,000 strong force disbanded once a promise to address their grievances had been received from the king, only for him to imprison and execute Aske the following year.

The ruthless defeat of the rebels encouraged Henry and Cromwell to dissolve the remaining monasteries, especially in the light of the involvement of the larger houses in the Pilgrimage. By using bribes, threats, fraud, and execution, or by placing their own puppet abbots in place to initiate closure, they managed by 1540 – when Waltham Abbey became the last house to be dissolved – to remove more than nine hundred years of monasticism from the face of England.

Henry gained much wealth from the venture, his Court of Augmentations receiving well over a million pounds by the end of his reign, yet by then he had wasted most of it in wars with France and Scotland. His son, as Edward VI, continued on a more zealous Protestant route but his premature death in 1553 allowed his Catholic stepsister Mary to try and reverse her predecessors' work, restoring Westminster as an abbey and commencing the building of a new charterhouse at Sheen. Little was achieved in her short reign and Elizabeth I, who succeeded her in 1559, re-established the Church of England.

▓ THE FATE OF THE MONKS

Some abbots had seen the dissolution coming and had prepared themselves financially. Those who gave up easily were well compensated with a pension of £100 per annum and the chance of high office in the new Church of England. Those who resisted (probably about half of the total number of nearly 850 houses that existed prior to dissolution) faced terrible retribution, like at Reading Abbey, where the abbot held out staunchly before being hanged, drawn and quartered despite being on good terms with the king.

Canons and friars who were also priests often found new positions in parishes, while younger monks frequently learned new trades, got married and vanished into secular society. The oldest monks, with only small pensions to rely on, were more likely to have been heard reminiscing of the good old days, that is if they could master the art of conversation after a lifetime of virtual silence.

The Abbey after the Dissolution

The closure of an abbey or priory usually resulted in an immediate and thorough raiding of its riches. Any valuables like silver plate and altar furniture were sent to the King's Wardrobe, useful metals like the bells and brasses went to the armories, while the lead off the roofs was melted down into ingots bearing the king's mark. Demolition, especially of the church, was usually swift, not only to gain a quick profit but also to render it unusable should the tide turn against Henry. Religious houses located in towns and cities were the most likely to be built over and today just an odd gatehouse, monastic building or place-name may survive to mark where an abbey once stood. Some sites were saved from destruction, though what part was retained depended upon its role prior to dissolution and the requirements of the new owners.

FIG 6.3: WESTMINSTER ABBEY, LONDON: *The west front of this notable landmark, dating mainly from the 13th–15th century, with the two towers in the picture added in the 18th century. Although dissolved in 1540, it was restored in 1556 by the Catholic Queen Mary, only to be suppressed again in 1560 by her sister, Elizabeth. The monks who fled this second time founded a monastery on the Continent. Their successors returned to these shores in the wake of the French Revolution and in 1802 established Ampleforth in Yorkshire, the largest monastery in England today.*

▨ THE CATHEDRAL PRIORIES

The association of a monastic community on the same site as the bishop's seat goes back to the Saxon period and a number of these cathedral priories lasted throughout the medieval period. At the dissolution the monastic buildings simply became accommodation for the new dean and chapter. Cathedrals standing today that once had priories include Canterbury, Rochester, Winchester, Worcester, Ely, Norwich, Carlisle and Durham.

▨ NEW CATHEDRALS

With the establishment of the Church of England there was a reorganisation of dioceses, and new cathedrals were required, with a number of old monastic churches being selected to fulfil the role of bishop's seat. The cathedrals you can visit today which were originally abbeys and became cathedrals at this time include Gloucester, Chester, Peterborough and Westminster, although the latter reverted to an abbey in Mary's reign.

▨ PARISH CHURCHES

Some parishes had the right to use part of a monastic church prior to the dissolution. Where this occurred the practice could continue, although the section used by the monks was often demolished, as at Croyland (see fig 5.11). In other situations the parishioners could purchase the site

FIG 6.4: BINHAM PRIORY, NORFOLK: *After this Benedictine priory was dissolved in 1539 the east end, tower and aisles were demolished, leaving this truncated nave as a parish church. The west end is notable as having one of the earliest examples of a bar tracery window, dating from 1244, although most of the window is now bricked in.*

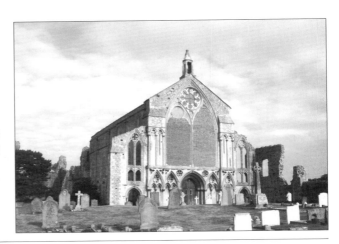

and use the abbey church as their own, which saved Tewkesbury Abbey among others (see fig 3.15). As the choir and presbytery were no longer required, the east end of the building was often destroyed or left to ruin, leaving a rather odd shaped, truncated nave as at Malmesbury (see fig 5.13).

Other communities found that the separate churches that the abbeys had often built for the local lay population were still sufficient and so the main monastic church and buildings were demolished. This occurred, for instance, at Bury St Edmunds, Reading, Much Wenlock and Whitby.

▨ COUNTRY HOUSES

It is likely that the majority of sites were granted to, or purchased by, new wealthy families looking for a country seat, Henry's favoured courtiers, or the officials who were responsible for overseeing the dissolution itself. They would have intended to use the site for a new house, but were probably cautious in the first few decades after the dissolution not to sink too much into the project in case there was a return to the Catholic faith, as was

threatened in Mary's reign. Some buildings would have been converted and the cloister or abbot's lodgings reused, with gardens established around this new secular residence. Many of the earthworks which today surround the ruins of abbeys may be the remains of these garden schemes, abandoned sometime later when a new house was built on a different site. Lacock Abbey, an Augustinian nunnery, was purchased by William Sharington and the house he built over the cloisters still survives today.

By the second half of the 16th century a more confident and secure aristocracy was rejecting medieval defensive planning and erecting grand, outward looking houses with prominent symmetrical façades filled with glass and the latest in Renaissance decoration. The Gothic abbeys they had purchased must have soon looked out of date, and from this period through to the 19th century they began building on new sites, usually raiding what was left of the monastic buildings for materials. At many country houses it is only the name – Woburn Abbey, for example, or Nostell Priory – that records the existence of a monastery.

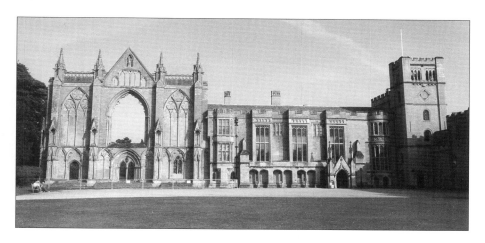

FIG 6.5: NEWSTEAD ABBEY, NOTTINGHAMSHIRE: *Originally a priory, which after the dissolution was converted into a dwelling. The west end of the church still stands in the left of this view, with the house built around its cloisters on the right.*

FIG 6.6: FOUNTAINS HALL, NORTH YORKSHIRE: *This Elizabethan mansion was erected from 1598–1604 using stone from the adjacent Fountains Abbey. The symmetry, the large mass of windows, Renaissance details, and its outward looking front are in stark contrast to the inward facing medieval buildings, which may have sufficed as the residence of a noble at the dissolution but now seemed outdated.*

Even this is not foolproof, though, as some houses known as 'Abbey' or 'Priory' were only monastic estates and not religious houses, while titles like 'Grange' (originally a monastic farm) were popular in the Victorian period on properties with no religious connections.

ROMANTIC RUINS

Fortunately, a number of abbeys, most notably those of the Cistercian Order,

were hidden away in remote valleys out of site of Protestant extremists and often protected by old Catholic families who still revered the sacred remains. In the second half of the 18th century the aristocracy sought to recreate their new found love for the picturesque in their own gardens by sprinkling a selection of ruined structures around their newly landscaped parks. Better still, though, was to have a real ruined abbey within their

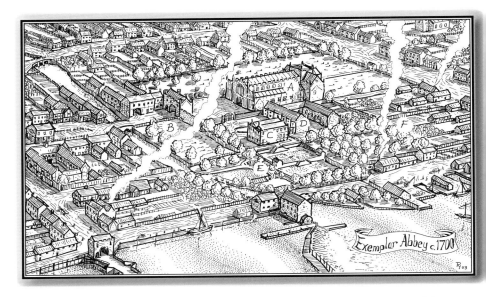

FIG 6.7: EXEMPLAR ABBEY c1700: *This final snapshot over our imaginary abbey is viewed 160 years after it was dissolved. The huge church (A) was retained for the use of the parish but the unused parts were demolished along with their old church at the gatehouse (B). The new owner of the monastic precinct has erected a mansion (C) and used parts of the old abbot's house and refectory to form his stable courtyard (D). Some of the old abbey fishponds (E) are now lakes within his formal garden, while the rest of the site was sold off for individual house plots (F). If we viewed the site today it is likely that much of this would in turn have gone, with only the church, probably restored in the 19th century, remaining along with the gatehouse. The only other reminder of the abbey could be local street and place names and the outline of the precinct, which could still show up as a property boundary or feature on a map.*

grounds, so those exceptional sites that had survived the last two centuries, like Fountains Abbey, became a central part of a garden scheme, or in the case of Rievaulx and Tintern abbeys, notable tourist attractions.

◼ NEW MONASTERIES

At the same time as these ruined medieval abbeys began to be appreciated for their picturesque qualities, there was growing tolerance of the old religion, culminating in the Catholic Emancipation Act of 1829. Refugees from the French Revolution had already quietly established a number of new monasteries and by the mid 19th century these were even joined by some Church of England foundations. Today, there are various abbeys and nunneries the length and breadth of the country, some noted for schools like Ampleforth in Yorkshire, others for enterprises like the pottery at Prinknash in Gloucestershire, although all but two of these are on new sites.

SECTION
II

THE ABBEY
IN
DETAIL

CHAPTER 7

The Church

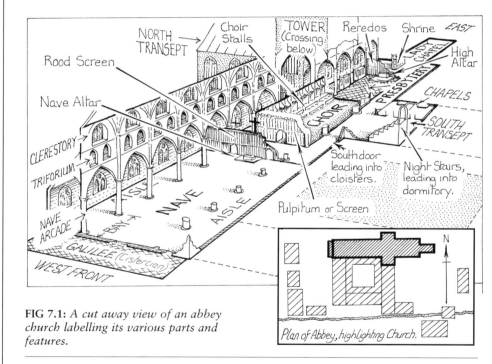

FIG 7.1: *A cut away view of an abbey church labelling its various parts and features.*

Plan of Abbey, highlighting Church.

The abbey church is invariably the most striking feature within monastic ruins. Whether it is the huge limestone walls perforated by rows of arched windows as at Rievaulx or the tall, jagged structure that commands the clifftops above the town of Whitby, it is the church that tends to draw our attention. Their massive size and dominance at most sites are a reflection of their importance to the monks, whose principal aim in life was the service of God.

The abbey church had a number of roles to fulfil. The central and east end containing the quire (choir) and presbytery were the sanctuary of the monks, usually referred to as quire monks to differentiate them from the more numerous lay brothers and

FIG 7.2: ST ALBANS CATHEDRAL, HERTFORDSHIRE: *Abbey churches were colourful places, as this medieval wall painting shows. Much of this artwork, whitewashed over during the fervent Protestantism of the late 16th and 17th centuries, was only uncovered when enthusiastic Victorian restorers stripped away the top surface.*

servants, who, if they did not have a separate place of worship, would use the west end of the church (nave). It was also the backdrop for processions, an important part of monastic life. These took place weekly and on special days, with the whole community forming a column which wound its way, though the complex, blessing altars along the way before the singing of High Mass. The medieval abbey church could be a highly decorated and colourful place, far from the plain bleached walls we see today.

The building was usually sited to the north of the cloister, to shield the compound in winter, although it is on the south at a few abbeys, due to limitations of the site or as in the case of Chester (fig 6.1) to keep out the noise of the town. By the Norman period the cruciform plan that the majority used had its long body carefully aligned on an east-west axis. Most churches were built over a long period of time, so the east end was always started first to allow services to be held in front of the high altar before the remainder was completed, a presumably draughty experience!

◾ THE WEST FRONT

This important front was the public face of the church and as the ceremonial entrance it was highly decorated, although

FIG 7.3: RIEVAULX ABBEY, NORTH YORKSHIRE: *The nearest, low stone walls in this view are of the galilee built against the west front, the higher wall just behind it. The tall structure in the right hand background is the east end of the same church, emphasising its huge scale.*

the way in for everyday visitors was a more discreet doorway, usually on the north side. The west front typically had a central, deeply recessed doorway, often with smaller openings on either side. There were either decorative bands of arcading or just a window above; early types of the latter had tall lancets and round openings (see fig 4.9), which were often replaced by a single massive window from the mid 13th century (see fig 6.4). The empty recesses that can often be found decorating this face originally held statues of saints and holy men, although most were destroyed during the Reformation and Commonwealth period.

Cistercian abbeys had a special porch built in front of the west doorway, known as a galilee (or occasionally a narthex). It is assumed that this was a covered assembly point for ceremonial processions and was named thus as the abbot at the head of the column of monks was compared to Jesus leading the disciples into Galilee. In most cases it was a long structure leaning up against the west wall with a single sloping roof and an open colonnade to the front. Some formed larger vestibules with vaulted ceilings and occasionally a chapel.

◉ THE NAVE

From the Latin word *navis*, meaning ship, the nave was the large west half of the church, which carried the congregation and in the Middle Ages was separated from the east end by screens. Larger structures had aisles that could be used as passageways behind the arcade of columns or piers supporting the tall walls of the nave. Above were one or two rows of arches; the middle one, where it existed, was called the triforium, its openings illuminating a passage running behind, and the top row of windows, which cast additional light upon the nave, was called the clerestory.

The huge height and length of some naves in monastic churches was for the formation and easy movement of ceremonial processions rather than to

FIG 7.4: MALMESBURY ABBEY, WILTSHIRE: *The interior of the nave showing the three levels of the wall: the arcade of columns and arches along the bottom (with the aisle behind), the next up being the triforium, and finally the clerestory on the top, which let in additional light. In some large and most smaller churches the triforium was omitted.*

FIG 7.5: *A drawing showing a niche cut into a nave column where a statue was once placed. These are often in association with an altar inserted after the lay brothers' stalls were removed in the late 14th century.*

hold a large number of worshippers. At a number of abbeys and priories, especially those of the Benedictines and Canons Regular, the local population had parish rights to the church and parts of the nave were provided for services. In a Cistercian monastery it was where the lay brothers sat during services, on stalls built between the columns of the arcade, with a rood screen (named after the crucifix which stood on top) cutting off the east end. When the numbers of lay brothers plummeted in the 14th century the nave was usually opened up and the stalls were removed, with additional altars sometimes

sited in their place. Niches in columns above where altars once stood and sockets and grooves in the masonry where the stalls and screens were fixed can still be found today.

◪ TOWER AND TRANSEPTS

The centre of the cruciform plan was usually marked by a tower, which not only housed the great bells but also structurally held the building together. The weight of its masonry counteracted the pressure from the four arms, and if it was not of sufficient bulk it could cause collapse, as happened with a number of Norman lantern towers which were too light. The architecturally austere Cistercians originally only permitted squat towers with just one bell, yet by the 15th century they were raising huge new structures, usually on the west end of the church and containing numerous bells. Larger churches of the other orders sometimes endowed this public end with pairs of towers. As well as holding the belfry, many Saxon structures and later those belonging to houses close to the disruptive borders of Scotland and Wales were used as look-outs and even last ditch defensive points, like the keep on a castle.

The area in the church directly below a central tower is called the crossing and is confined between the four massive piers or columns that supported the structure above (today the footings that remain of these will usually be wider than those that held up the church walls). The two short arms either side of the crossing, the north and south transepts, completed the cruciform plan and were used to create extra space for altars. From the south transept ran a set of stairs up to the dormitory, so monks could come directly into the church for the night service. These doorways can still be found today – left stranded high up on the south wall.

Bells were essential to the efficient running of the monastery, where individual monks had no watches or clocks to tell the time and the rules of silence prevented calling out loud to summon them. Monks in fact were among the first to develop mechanical clocks, some to wake them for night offices, others to strike a bell for the hours during the day. One complex example from the 1320s was erected at St Albans and was one of the first public clocks in the country. The great bells housed in the tower were principally rung to mark the hours (the services which were sung at specified times through the day and night) and would have echoed out down the valley or across the fields, while smaller bells on other buildings around the cloister signalled lesser daily events. So loud were the bells at Rievaulx that the monks of nearby Byland Abbey moved further away so as not to be confused by their ringing.

QUIRE/CHOIR

The quire or choir was the place in the heart of the church where the monks sat to chant the hours, the eight services that made up the divine order or opus Dei (God's Work) for each day. The first was matins, at the seemingly unholy hour of 2 am, and this was followed by lauds and prime before many of us would have even thought of rising today. The work of the day was broken by three further visits to the quire for terce, sext and nones, while the evening services of vespers and compline were completed around 7.30 pm

FIG 7.6: VALLE CRUCIS ABBEY, CLWYD: *The south transept of the church, showing the doorway, stranded up on the wall, which led into the dormitory; the night stairs that ran down below it have long since gone (see also fig 8.7).*

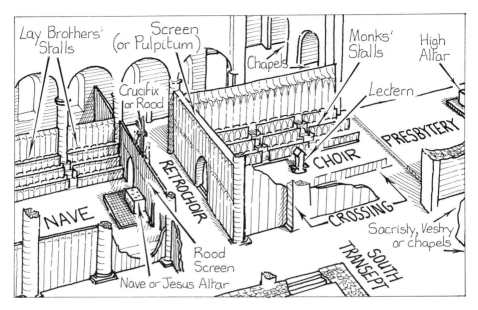

Lay Brothers' Stalls

Screen (or Pulpitum)

Monks' Stalls

High Altar

Chapels

Crucifix or Rood

Lectern

RETROCHOIR

PRESBYTERY

CHOIR

NAVE

CROSSING

Sacristy, Vestry or chapels

Rood Screen

SOUTH TRANSEPT

Nave or Jesus Altar

FIG 7.7: *A drawing showing the central part of the church with the east end of the nave and the choir in the area of the crossing.*

in winter and 8.30 pm in summer. We all know how onerous listening to a service can be – the poor monks not only had to do it eight times a day but had strict rules of decency which prohibited conversation, smiling, and even crossing or stretching their legs.

The choir itself usually stretched from the crossing up into the east end of the church, although the pulpitum (the Latin word for platform or scaffold), which shut off its west end, could stretch back into the nave. From the late 12th century the east ends of churches were often extended, one reason being to move the quire further away from the nave to increase privacy. The quire was open to the altar on the east side and enclosed on the north and south by wooden screens, which in the Norman churches could have been decorated with

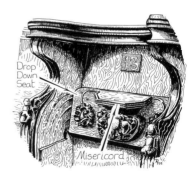

Drop Down Seat

Misericord

FIG 7.8: *A drawing of part of the choir stalls showing a misericord on the upturned back of the chair.*

blind arcading (see fig 3. 11) but from the turn of the 14th century more typically had canopied recesses, a number of which survive today. Parallel to these were the monks' stalls, which ascended on either side of a central walkway with a lectern in the middle, on which the music books were supported. Monks were expected to stand through much of the services, so to make the hours of chanting more bearable wooden ledges were fitted to the underside of their chairs, so as they rose and flipped up the seats they could lean back onto the projection for support. These are called misericords – which means 'mercy'!

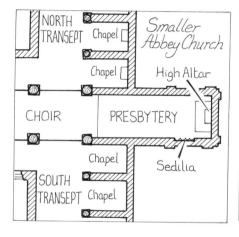

FIG 7.9:*Two plans showing the possible arrangement you could find in the east end of an early or small abbey church (above) and a later or large one (right).*

PRESBYTERY

The word, meaning 'priest's place', was applied to the east end of the church beyond the choir. The presbytery could vary from a short, narrow, walled enclosure to a spacious area bounded by aisles and magnificent windows. Early types often had a semicircular eastern end (apse), some with smaller but similar shaped chapels set around it, while examples from the mid 12th century onwards tend to be longer and rectangular in plan. The division between the presbytery and the choir was marked by a single step, which often survives in ruins today and leads onto the centre of the presbytery (also known as the sanctuary). Here stood the high altar, either on the east wall (once the priests took mass in front of it rather than behind from the 12th century) or forward from it, on a stone screen called a reredos. The area around was usually tiled, a luxury flooring in the medieval period, often produced by abbeys themselves, like Chertsey in Surrey, examples from which can be found in the British Museum.

On the south wall a number of recesses

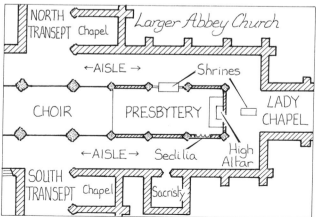

**FIG 7.11:
FURNESS ABBEY,
CUMBRIA:** *A
highly ornamental
sedilia. Early
types may have
had simple arched
recesses but
examples like this
with decorated
canopies above
date from the
14th and 15th
centuries.*

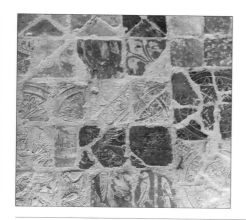

FIG 7.10: *Medieval tiles, which usually paved the area around the altars, although you may find them reset elsewhere today. From left to right they are from Thornton Abbey, Humberside, Byland Abbey, North Yorkshire, and Buildwas Abbey, Shropshire.*

were provided for use during services. A sedilia (from the Latin *sedile*, a seat) is a set of stone seats cut out of the wall for officials to use during mass. There are usually three in number, but sometimes more, which step up, with the most senior member sitting highest at the end nearest the altar. Nearby would be a piscina (a general name for a pool, from the Latin *piscis*, meaning fish), which in this situation was a stone basin with a drain, sometimes supported on a column, used for rinsing out the communion vessels. There would also be a credence, which was a shelf on which the bottles of wine and water were placed. An aumbry was a small square cupboard, a few feet across, which was recessed into the wall, with locking doors to protect holy relics and other valuables. Although the wooden doors have long since gone, the square holes still remain, sometimes with hinge sockets to the side.

Shrines were housed in this most sacred part of the church. In early churches they were usually in the basement or crypt underneath the presbytery and viewed by pilgrims from an ambulatory, which ran around the outside of it with separate entrances and exits to cope with a flood

of visitors. In the 13th century many abbeys were encouraged to dust down their sacred relics and saintly remains and provide them with a new setting upstairs, either to the side of the sanctuary or in the place of highest honour directly behind the high altar. The income from pilgrims usually made any new building a worthwhile endeavour, especially to the relic-obsessed Benedictines, and their value was such that watching lofts were sometimes built for the monks who had to guard them day and night. Most relics and remains were collected by Henry VIII at the dissolution, for example the famous Holy Blood from Hailes Abbey in Gloucestershire, which had financed the rebuilding of the church in the 13th century but which was now claimed by the Crown to be no more than animals' blood changed each week by the monks.

CHAPELS

A growing number of these small rooms off the main church were erected around the presbytery and east side of the transepts to house altars for the increasing numbers of monks becoming priests and in response to the rising popularity of the

FIG 7.12: GLOUCESTER CATHEDRAL, GLOUCESTER: *When Edward II was uneremoniously put to death by conspirators inserting a red hot poker up his nether regions, the abbot of the Benedictine abbey at Gloucester moved quickly to acquire his remains. The shrine that was erected on the north side of the high altar under the instructions of Edward III became a popular and lucrative possession, the pillars on either side being cut back so that pilgrims could move around it.*

private mass. Other altars were provided at certain locations within the church, and some could also be found elsewhere – in the infirmary, chapter house, guest accommodation or gatehouse. The most important was the Lady chapel, which was dedicated to the Virgin Mary and found popularity from the 12th century. It was often sited as an extension behind the east wall, its structure helping to support this face, while others were built on the north or south side of the presbytery. Cistercian houses did not have them as their whole church was dedicated to her already. The remains of chapels today may house similar features to the presbytery, notably the base where the altar stood and perhaps a piscina or aumbry.

The Cloister Buildings

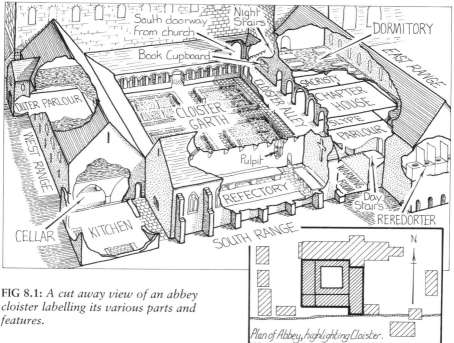

FIG 8.1: *A cut away view of an abbey cloister labelling its various parts and features.*

Plan of Abbey, highlighting Cloister.

If the monks' spiritual needs were fulfilled within the church, then their physical requirements were satisfied within the buildings that surrounded the cloister. This was a roughly square area comprising a central open area called the garth, which was bounded on all four sides by a covered alley (cloister comes from the Latin *claustrum* which means enclosed space). The buildings that enclosed the cloister were in similar positions throughout the medieval period, with only slight variations due to the particular demands of a religious order or an awkward site.

Although the alleys were used as sheltered passages connecting each of the rooms, they were also important as a place

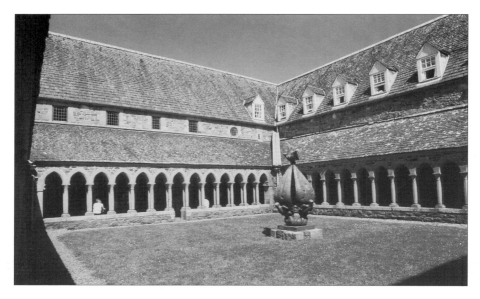

FIG 8.2: IONA ABBEY, OFF THE ISLE OF MULL: *A view of the restored cloister with an open arcade, showing how it may have looked in the 12th or 13th century (the dormer windows in the roof are much later and the garth in the middle would have been a garden).*

for peace and meditation. The north alley, which ran alongside the church nave, was divided up on its garden side by wooden screens creating small cubicles, usually with a desk, called carrels, in which the monks could pray, study and read. Cistercians had a collation seat along the wall of this passage, on which the abbot would sit during his evening reading (the collation). The alleys themselves may have been simple timber lean-to structures in the first monasteries to use a cloister (probably from the 10th century in England), but the remains that survive today had later arches of stone set on a low wall, which from the 14th century may have been partly or fully glazed.

The garth was purely ornamental and was probably divided up by paths with beds between filled with flowers, herbs, trees or lawn. Occasionally there may have been a water feature, such as a laver in some Cluniac priories (see fig 8.10) or towers from which water was distributed to individual cells in Carthusian houses. This order was also unique in burying their deceased monks within the garth, a rather morbid thought to us today but to the Carthusians it must have been a reminder of the glory that awaited them on the other side, to help them through the rigour of their strictly ascetic life.

◼ LIBRARY, SACRISTRY AND VESTRY

This chapter follows a clockwise journey around a typical cloister as illustrated in fig 8.1, starting as you step out of the abbey church by the south door. This entrance was usually decorated and featured bands of receding arches as it was an important access through which the processions passed. The first feature you may come across on your left is an open wall recess. This was a book cupboard, which originally would have had wooden doors and shelves, and was conveniently placed at one end of the north cloister alley where the monks sat in their carrels to study. In the later Middle Ages, as the better educated monks required more books, a small library was provided, often between the church and the chapter house.

This same spot might also be used for a sacristy or vestry, the former used to house the sacred vessels and stores used in the church, the latter for holding the church vestments (in some situations the rooms may have been combined in one). These rooms, which were under the supervision of a sacristan, could be positioned off one of the transepts or the north aisle of the church, but sometimes they were trapped between the south transept and chapter house, although as direct access was always required into the church an additional door was knocked through into it.

▣ CHAPTER HOUSE

The most important room off the east alley, and second only in importance to the church, was the chapter house, where the abbot and the monks held a daily meeting, typically around 8 am. Here they could discuss the running of the abbey and its estates, hear confessions and decide upon punishments, read the notices of the dead and the lists of the monks' duties. Each gathering began with a reading of a chapter from the Rule of St Benedict, hence the name of the room.

The entrance is usually marked by three arched openings, often stunningly dec-

orated with radiating bands of voussoirs and carvings, the central one leading into the chapter house (in Cistercian houses the two flanking arches often served as libraries). As this was a two-storey range and an important room, the ceiling was usually vaulted in stone, and in larger examples it would have one or two rows of columns in the middle to support it. The monks sat on stone benches around the walls, with the abbot having his seat in the middle of the east wall (there may be a gap today where this would have been). This sacred room was also the resting place for

FIG 8.3: LILLESHALL ABBEY, SHROPSHIRE: *A book cupboard built into the wall to the right of the south doorway into the church. The horizontal grooves inside were for shelves, while the two openings are recessed to take doors, with the triangular block in between them fitted to take a locking bolt.*

FIG 8.4: HAUGHMOND ABBEY, SHROPSHIRE: *The late 12th century triple arched opening in front of the chapter house, richly decorated to proclaim its important status. The interior was rebuilt around 1500 and the square headed window and font were probably fitted here around this time.*

the heads of the monastery and the grave slabs of past abbots can still be seen in their original or re-sited positions within the remains of chapter houses today.

Early chapter houses tend to be in a rectangular room beneath the dormitory, although in many abbeys they project outwards to the east to make them large enough to hold the community. Later, ambitious houses who wanted a more glorious structure were restricted by the floor above, so they usually repositioned it behind this range with the former room becoming a vestibule leading to it. Now they could construct a taller, freestanding building either in the traditional rectangular shape or to a polygonal plan.

▧ SLYPE AND INNER PARLOUR

Access would be required from the cloister and its rooms through to the infirmary and the monks' cemetery behind them to the east. The slype was a covered passageway which ran through this range, sometimes to the north of the chapter house but, especially in Cistercian houses often on its south side, as they usually put the sacristy or library on the other side (as in fig 8.1). It would have originally had lockable doors at both ends and sometimes stone seating or decorative arcading along its walls. The inner parlour (from the French verb *parler*, meaning 'to speak') was a place where the rule of silence was relaxed and necessary conversation, usually prior to a chapter meeting, could take place. It was either a separate room, a passage running alongside the slype or combined with the latter as a single passage. It was through this that the body of a deceased monk was transported to the cemetery after the funeral service had been held in the chapter house.

▣ DORMITORY AND REREDORTER

Running the length of the first floor above the former listed rooms in the eastern range would usually be the dormitory or dorter (except in Carthusian houses, where the monks slept in their own cells). This was the sleeping quarters for the quire monks and would have originally been a long, open plan hall with crude beds probably made from straw pallets or filled mattresses laid out along the main walls. They would have slept with their habits still on and would only have removed any outer garments and their knives in case of an accident during a particularly restless night's sleep. As conditions improved, especially from the 14th century, fireplaces appeared along the wall and the dorter was divided up by wood panelling, creating private cubicles, which might feature a desk, cupboard and preferably a window. As this was a first floor room it is less likely

FIG 8.5: FOUNTAINS ABBEY, NORTH YORKSHIRE: *The interior of the chapter house looking towards the three arches at the west end. The monks' seats still survive in part along the side walls, as do higher up the corbels (stone brackets), which along with the columns, the bases of which survive on the floor, supported the stone vaulted ceiling. On the floor are grave slabs that covered the burials of former abbots.*

FIG 8.6: THORNTON ABBEY, HUMBERSIDE: *A freestanding, octagonal chapter house, built behind the east range and dating from extensive rebuilding of the abbey in the late 13th and early 14th centuries. There would have originally been a pier in the centre, supporting the roof.*

to have survived than the rooms below, although the impression of its roofline can often be seen where it butted up to the outside of the south transept (see fig 4.1). Where dorters do survive, expect to see a row of low, thin windows on their exposed walls (see fig 8.7).

The abbot may have originally slept alongside his fellow monks but even from an early date he moved to the most comfortable area of the dorter (nearest to the warming house), or to a separate room linked to the sleeping quarters by a passage. In most houses by the 14th century the abbot could expect his own

lodgings elsewhere in the complex.

At the end wall butting up to the church a door led to the night stairs. A light would have always been lit within the dorter for the monks when they rose in the night and descended the stairs for services. At the opposite end or along the side wall would have been a door or passage leading to the reredorter (simply meaning room at the rear) which was the monks' toilet. Cleanliness was of prime importance in a monastery and elaborate systems of drainage and water channelling were devised, with their position often determining the layout of the buildings, in

FIG 8.7: VALLE CRUCIS ABBEY, CLWYD: *An exterior view (above) of the east range from the cloister garth, with the row of narrow windows on the upper floor marking the dormitory. The interior (below) was once partitioned, with fireplaces (one still open and others blocked) along the right hand wall. The opening at the far end led to the night stairs and into the church (see fig 7.6).*

FIG 8.8: FURNESS ABBEY, CUMBRIA: *The twin channels in the foreground ran under the reredorter, which was built over them (the low walls on each side) so that effluent would drop directly into the water. It was connected by a bridge to the dormitory on the left (note the narrow windows), the white crumbled wall in between being one of the buttresses built later to stop its east wall from leaning over.*

particular the reredorter. This had a row of partitioned seats with holes inset against the rear wall and was positioned directly above the flowing water so the effluent was carried straight off the site.

◼ WARMING HOUSE OR CALEFACTORIUM

Life for the monks during winter must have been intolerably bitter, with no heating and little to keep out the draughts. A small concession was the warming house, a single room with a fireplace, in which they could thaw out for a short period (the only other places where a fire was permitted were the kitchen and the infirmary). It was usually positioned under the dormitory, near where it meets the south range, or, especially in Cistercian houses, it was further round, next to the refectory. The fire was lit on All Saints'

Day and remained burning for about five months up to Good Friday. When in the later 14th century the monks had fireplaces in their dormitory, the warming house often became a heated common room, used for small gatherings or celebrations.

◼ REFECTORY OR FRATER

Turning to the south range, opposite the church, you come across the refectory or frater, which tends to occupy the greater part of its length. Before entering, the monks would have washed their hands using a laver, a lead-lined stone trough filled with water, which was usually built into the wall on one or both sides of this entrance or occasionally positioned as a freestanding basin in the corner of the cloister garth. Where these survive today you can often make out the holes for the pipes where the water would have entered (commonly through a decorative lion's head or some form of tap) and the drain leading off at an angle from the base. There may also be a stone recess to one side, which was used as a cupboard to hold the towels for drying the monks' hands.

The refectory in which the monks took their meals was a long hall open to the rafters, either on the ground floor or raised above an undercroft (a basement), which was used as a cellar. The entrance was usually towards the west end, with long tables and benches lined along the sides and in larger examples another row or two parallel to them in the middle. At the east end and at right angles to the others was the high table, perhaps on a raised platform called a dais, at which the abbot or prior and his selected guests would have sat, with a cross or painted scene on the wall above them. Up along the side wall furthest from the church would have been a pulpit accessed by a stone staircase built into the wall, from which a different member of the community each week would have read out aloud a portion of scripture from a book which was often kept in an aumbry near the entrance to the stairs. At the west

FIG 8.9: FOUNTAINS ABBEY, NORTH YORKSHIRE: *The warming room with a huge fireplace around which the shivering monks would have gathered for warmth. The horizontal lintel above it is rare, only held in place by clever cutting of the stonework, although a wooden frame has been inserted today to avoid collapse.*

FIG 8.10: MUCH WENLOCK PRIORY, SHROPSHIRE: *The circular laver or lavabo in the foreground is sited in the corner of the cloister garth, with the ruins of the church in the background. It was originally enclosed by an octagonal building (see the low walls around it) and had three tiers of water tanks on top of it.*

end there might be a hatch through which the food was served and brought to the tables by servitors, who along with the reader and cooks would have taken their meals later.

Cistercian abbeys often turned the refectory 90° so that its shorter entrance end faced onto the cloister. This would mean that its length was not limited by the width of the cloister, but more importantly it permitted the kitchen to be sited in the gap created between it and the west range, where their lay brethren also took their meals – a convenient arrangement which meant that meals could be served through hatches directly into each refectory.

The remains of refectories can still give an impression of their former glory, some retaining the large windows along the side (see fig 6.2), which by the 14th century could have held colourful heraldic glass with the coats of arms of benefactors. The stone bases of the tables and benches are often found within, and the base of the stairs leading to the pulpit can survive when the walls themselves are all but gone.

▧ KITCHEN

The kitchen was logically sited near to the refectory, yet its noisy environment and the potential risk of burning down the abbey from its open fireplace meant that it was often a freestanding structure sited to the rear of the south or west range and connected by a covered passageway. Cistercians tended to put the kitchen between the monks' frater and the west range, where their lay brothers ate, so that food could be served directly to both areas through hatches. It is likely that you will find other kitchens around an abbey site; one is usually positioned next to the infirmary and others may have been built at a later date for the abbot's own lodgings or a guest house. Vegetables formed the basis of the monks' diet and cauldrons would have simmered over fireplaces or raised stoves, while a number of sinks and tanks would have been used for washing or storing them. At a later date as the rules were relaxed, some meat was consumed and separate kitchens featuring large open

ranges were built to supply a dining room known as a misericord (see Chapter 9).

Most kitchens were rectangular structures, usually with a pantry, buttery or scullery, and an outer courtyard where fuel and other stores may have been kept. Some were grand structures with a square or polygonal plan, covered by a large conical roof with ornate openings at the crest. These louvres were originally fitted at the apex of roofs to let the smoke out but later ones tended to have large open cooking ranges built into walls with chimneys above. The footings of these, often lined with brick or tiles and built within the walls or as structures in the middle, can frequently be found, along with round baking ovens, stone sinks and serving hatches in the walls.

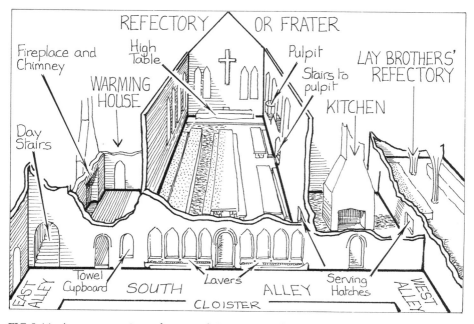

FIG 8.11: *A cut-away view of a typical Cistercian refectory and the adjoining buildings.*

FIG 8.12: LEISTON ABBEY, SUFFOLK: *The ruins of the refectory with its large west window. It is built parallel to the south of the cloister, to be seen in the right of this picture.*

FIG 8.13: GLASTONBURY ABBEY, SOMERSET: *This square structure with a tall pointed roof is a rare example of a medieval kitchen.*

◈ WEST OR CELLARER'S RANGE

The only universal purpose for the west range of the cloister was to complete the enclosure, the specific use for it being decided after it was built and varying even between houses of the same order. It was a two-storey structure with the bottom level having a stone vaulted ceiling, a convenient place in many monasteries for a cellar housing much of the food produced within the abbey precinct or delivered from outside. As this range also faced outwards onto the great court, which was the public entrance to the abbey, a parlour where the monks (especially the cellarer) could meet and talk with traders was usually sited nearest the church. There may have also been a porch on this western front with an office or checker above for the cellarer, in which he kept the abbey accounts (calculation was made upon a checked board or cloth, hence 'checker').

FIG 8.14: JERVAULX ABBEY, NORTH YORKSHIRE: *Many ruined abbeys have relics of the more mundane parts of the community sprinkled around the site. This is an example of a sink, which at the time were shallow basins carved out of blocks of stone.*

FIG 8.15: FOUNTAINS ABBEY, NORTH YORKSHIRE: *The spectacular stone vaulted cellarium running the length of the west range's ground floor. Originally, though, this was divided up with screens or walls, with the lay brothers' refectory where the shot is taken from, the cellar and a parlour for its official in the middle and the outer parlour at the far end.*

Cistercian abbeys used the west range to house the lay brethren, with their refectory usually in the southern end next to the kitchen and their dormitory above. As some of these abbeys had many hundreds to look after, the west range could extend southwards, becoming a huge structure divided up by screens and walls between cellar, parlour and frater. As lay brothers were less often present during the 14th century, other uses were found for this range, with it usually being divided up into separate rooms perhaps for guests or – as sometimes happened at Benedictine houses – as a hall and private chambers for the abbot.

CHAPTER 9

The Abbey Precinct

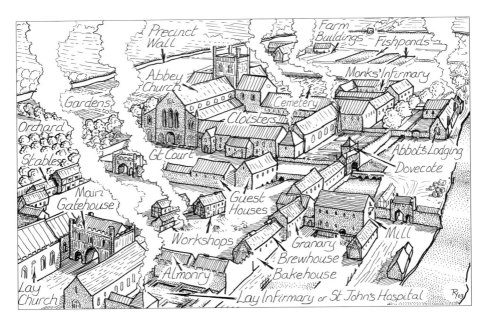

FIG 9.1: *A view over an imaginary abbey precinct showing some of the buildings that may have stood there, although a number are usually associated with one particular order so may not have appeared together as this view may imply.*

The dramatic ruins of abbey churches and cloisters set among lawns and fields today give a misleading impression that this was the monastery in its entirety. This stone enclosure was usually but a small core of a much larger complex set within the abbey precinct, which was bounded by a wall with at least one gatehouse commanding the entry points. The interior may have been subdivided into separate courts, an outer one often containing buildings associated with the production of food and materials for the abbey, and a great court usually to the west of the cloister where the guest house

FIG 9.2: FOUNTAINS ABBEY, NORTH YORKSHIRE: *The medieval watermill standing to the west of the famous abbey.*

was found. In a town location, where further expansion was limited, even powerful and rich abbeys had to fit their buildings within an area perhaps only a few hundred metres square. Groups like the Cistercians in remote locations had fewer restrictions and the surrounding wall could wander for up to two to three miles around huge enclosures.

The medieval abbey had to be relatively self-supporting, and therefore within the precinct there were all the departments required to maintain the abbey itself and support the monks and their guests. There were workshops, forges and masons' yards in which stone, timber and metalwork was produced for repairs or new structures. Barns and granaries were used to store corn and produce, livestock was held in animal pens, and horses in the stables. Freestanding dovecotes or spaces in lofts were common to provide pigeons and doves for the barren winter table. Fish

was another essential part of the monks' diet; so abbeys could hold fishing rights to parts of the nearby rivers, store salted sea fish, or build fishponds where coarse fish like pike and tench could be bred. Many of these farm type buildings and structures can also be found on the estates owned by the abbeys, which are covered in the next chapter.

In a time when water was often unsafe to drink, beer was consumed at most meals and even by nuns, so each abbey would have a brewhouse where typically a new batch, made from wheat or oats, was produced each week, with the poorest quality brew being sent to the almonry to be distributed to the needy. Bakehouses were also essential, to produce bread not only for the monks' table but also that of their guests and to be given away as alms. This building was often near a mill, which was usually powered by a waterwheel, as most sites were in valleys with good

**FIG 9.3:
THORNTON
ABBEY,
HUMBERSIDE:**
*The eastern
(inner) face of
this 14th century
gatehouse (see fig
5.2). The two
levels of rooms
above the
entrance arch
were luxuriously
fitted out for a
senior member of
the community
or important
guests.*

supplies of running water. There may have been more than one mill on some sites, used either for grinding grain or in some cases for fulling, the process of cleaning and thickening cloth.

In addition to the food stored in farm buildings, much of the monks' diet would have been produced in the gardens and orchards within the precinct. Fruits along with vegetables such as leeks, beans and peas were grown for the table, while herbs including pennyroyal for toothaches and lavender for pains in the head were supplied for the abbey pharmacy. The

almonry near the entrance to the site or the gatehouse itself were used for the distribution of alms, which each religious community was obliged to provide – from the simple handing over of food to education and accommodation.

As many of the above structures were timber-framed most have long since gone but occasional fragments and impressions do survive in a few abbey precincts. There are, however, a number of important buildings that are often found today amidst the monastic ruins or as the last surviving part on an urban site, the first of

FIG 9.4: EASBY ABBEY, NORTH YORKSHIRE: *The above view shows the exterior of this late 13th century gatehouse with the single large pointed arch. The left hand view shows the interior of the entry passage, with a dividing wall containing a large opening for carts and a smaller one for pedestrians to save opening the main gates for the more frequent foot traffic.*

these being the entrance to the abbey itself.

▨ THE GATEHOUSE AND PRECINCT WALL

Early medieval monasteries were probably bounded by ditches and banks surmounted by timber palisades (fences), with only modest gatehouses covering the entrance, as few wished to burn down the abbey in these times of the more revered monk. By the mid 13th century, as conflict became more common so did stone precinct walls and formidable gatehouses, although medieval restrictions on the mixing of military and religious matters meant that

FIG 9.5: ABINGDON ABBEY, OXFORDSHIRE: *This gateway dating from the mid 15th century (note the flat pointed arch and square headed surround) has the pedestrian entrance to the left in this picture; the porter's lodge originally on the right, was knocked through by the Victorians to make a symmetrical façade. The building to the left of the gateway is St Nicholas' church, which was built for abbey staff and travellers, while the lower part of the structure on the right is the remains of St John's Hospital, built to serve the lay community. Such hosipitals were a common feature of Benedictine abbeys.*

they tended to lack the extreme defensive features such as drawbridges and murder holes that were acceptable on castles.

Most surviving gatehouses date from the troubled 14th and 15th centuries and were built at least two storeys high, with a main passageway below, usually flanked on the right by a smaller door for pedestrians (so that the heavy main gate would not have to be opened just to let foot traffic through). There would have been a room to the side for the porter, while the other chambers, usually on the floors above, could be used for accommodation, chapels for those not permitted to enter (often for the laity at nunneries), prisons, courtrooms, almonries and schools. There may have also been additional smaller gateways covering other entrances or between different sections within the precinct itself.

Many monastic gatehouses still stand today, some long after the buildings they guarded have gone. At the dissolution the king's commissioners often encouraged the farmers who took over monastic sites to reuse the gatehouse as a farmhouse, and their practical size, substantial build and continuing use must also have helped them to survive.

FIG 9.6: DORCHESTER ABBEY, OXFORDSHIRE: *This much altered building standing directly to the west of the abbey church is believed to have been the guest house, although it was later a school and now houses a small local museum.*

◼ GUEST HOUSES OR HOSPICES

Monastic rules insisted upon the accommodation of visitors and all abbeys had some space set aside for this. It may have been a few chambers in one of the monastic buildings or a separate structure, and in larger monasteries it may have been either of these, depending on the importance of the guest. The freestanding houses are often found in the great court to the west of the cloister so that the noise of the coming and going of visitors would not disturb the monks within. They could be impressive structures with halls and chambers for the guests and stables outside for their horses.

◼ THE MONKS' INFIRMARY AND CEMETERY

The infirmary or farmery was an essential part of any monastery and was usually sited to the east of the cloister, away from the noisier west side of the precinct. It provided more comfortable accommodation for monks who had either fallen sick or were too old or infirm for their strict lifestyle and diet. There was usually a large hall with beds laid out, similar to a modern hospital ward, and a hearth in the middle, while later examples had more numerous fireplaces along the walls and wooden partitions creating individual cubicles for the patients. The infirmary

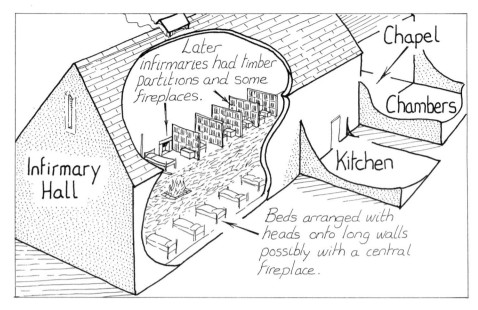

Later infirmaries had timber partitions and some fireplaces.

Chapel

Chambers

Infirmary Hall

Kitchen

Beds arranged with heads onto long walls possibly with a central fireplace.

Fig 9.7: *A cut-away drawing showing some of the features of an infirmary, although the positions of its parts are not based on any actual plan.*

would usually have a chapel, often at the east end of the hall, separate chambers for the master of the farmery and a kitchen, where, as part of the more lenient rules, meat could be cooked for inmates.

Monks would have also regularly visited the infirmary when recuperating after blood letting. Medieval medicine revolved around the four humours of the body: blood, yellow bile, phlegm and black bile, and it was believed that any excess of these would result in illness. It was therefore a popular practice to drain an amount of blood at periodic intervals (typically four to eight times a year) and let the 'minuti', as monks going through this process were known, recover in the more relaxed surroundings of the infirmary. In fact it became a bit of a problem, as monks seemed to have looked

forward to this event as a kind of holiday where they could be warm, talk and feast on meat, so some orders took measures to stop them undergoing excessive bleedings!

For those who did not recover it was just a short trip to the cemetery, which was usually laid out around the east of the abbey church or chapter house and to the north of the infirmary. Unlike a modern day cemetery there were no gravestones; the monks were buried without coffins in unmarked graves on an east-west alignment. There would have been access either via the slype or from the north of the church, sometimes with a small gateway in the stone wall that bounded the plot. The superiors of the religious houses were typically buried in stone coffins in the chapter house or occasionally the abbey church, where honoured lay benefactors may also have been privileged enough to be laid to rest. Their stone coffins and lids are often found in or near to these places today.

MISERICORD OR FARMERY FRATER

It was common for a separate eating area to be provided in the vicinity of the infirmary as meat could not be consumed in the main refectory. As rules on the consumption of meat relaxed in the 13th and 14th centuries, this building, often called a misericord (as with the ledge on choir seats – see Chapter 7 – because it was seen as 'merciful'), became frequented on certain days of the week by all the monks.

THE ABBOT'S LODGINGS

By the 13th and 14th centuries the superior of the house began to expect the same level of accommodation as those of similar standing in medieval society and they also of him. As a result abbots and priors increasingly converted rooms within the cloister buildings or erected a separate structure elsewhere within the precinct to provide them with a hall and private chambers. In many cases these were either extensions of the western range of the cloister or within the great court, except in Cistercian houses, where lay brothers used this side of the abbey, and the abbot's lodgings were usually positioned to the south or east depending upon the site.

FIG 9.8: CROXDEN ABBEY, STAFFORDSHIRE: *The ruins of the abbot's lodgings built in the 14th century to the south-east of the cloister.*

FIG 9.9: MOUNT GRACE PRIORY, NORTH YORKSHIRE: *A spring house covering one of the wells that provided drinking water to this Carthusian monastery. Most abbeys had some system of covered springs, settling tanks, pipes and channels inside and outside its precinct to protect and purify the supply.*

There would have been a main hall, often raised above a stone vaulted cellar or undercroft, with separate chambers leading off it, a private chapel and sometimes a separate kitchen. These buildings could be elaborate and were commonly used by the new owners immediately after the dissolution.

▣ WATER SUPPLY AND DRAINS

There are many stories associated with monasteries about tunnels leading from the precinct to secret locations around the neighbouring countryside or towns. Many of these local legends, though, probably come from colourful interpretations of the stone-lined passages that were found on monastic sites once they were opened up after the dissolution. Unfortunately, what were thought to be tunnels turn out to be just drains! The primary reason for the choice of site and the subsequent layout of the abbey revolved around the provision of water for drinking and flushing out the drains. The monks went to great lengths to build elaborate systems of channels, settling tanks and pipes to ensure a reliable supply of fresh water, which was distributed across the site to places such as the lavers and kitchens. Rivers and streams were also redirected down stone-lined channels to flush out the waste from the reredorters and kitchens.

FIG 9.10: HAUGHMOND ABBEY, SHROPSHIRE: *A stone-lined drain running along the side of the reredorter, the remains of which are on the left. The water appeared out of the tunnel at the far end and flushed the waste out of the site and into the river below.*

CHAPTER 10

Abbey Estates and Other Remains in the Landscape

FIG 10.1: GRANGE, BORROWDALE, LAKE DISTRICT:
*This idyllic hamlet set in the heart of the Lake District has, as its name
would suggest, its origins as a monastic grange of Furness Abbey, some
thirty miles to the south. This large Cistercian house acquired the estate
in the 13th century to add to its already impressive portfolio of land,
including some twenty other granges within ten miles of the site.
Like other estates across north-west England, it also possessed mills,
mines and numerous other properties in the local area.*

FIG 10.2: ROYSTON GRANGE, DERBYSHIRE: *High up on the south-east corner of the Peak District are many instances of 'Grange' marked on the map, including this well researched example. Although the buildings are more recent, some of the boundaries date back to the 12th century, when it was established as a monastic grange of Garendon Abbey. Walls like these which follow a curved line tend to be ancient and could either be where land has been scooped out of woodland (assarting), typically in the medieval period, or they date at least in plan from Roman or prehistoric times, when this site was known to have been used.*

My house on the edge of the Peak District overlooks a semi-wooded valley with open pasture along its level floor, where five hundred years ago Dieulacres Abbey stood. Although only scant remains of the monastic buildings exist today, within a private farm, there are a number of features in the surrounding landscape that were shaped by the Cistercians.

The river runs along the side of the valley, held back by a bank almost certainly created by the monks as part of their water control system and to increase the land available for farming. Stone from the abbey can be found on buildings in the vicinity, while the word 'Grange' appears on maps of the peaks to the east of the site, recording the agricultural estates run by this order.

All over the country there are buildings, earthworks, river channels, bridges and place-names that owe their presence to the medieval monk. This chapter looks at some of those that can still be found even in areas bereft of ruined abbeys.

▣ GRANGES

Monasteries relied financially upon the land they were granted at their foundation or had acquired over the years. Revenue came either in the form of rent for the use of the land, or from profit made on the agricultural produce, with some farmland, usually close to the monastery, retained to supply the monks' own table. When the Cistercians arrived and spread rapidly in the mid 12th century they brought with them a new way of running their estates. Land was grouped into convenient blocks and then a number of their lay brethren or conversi were sent to administer it from a farm complex that has become known as a grange (the most notable of these being the huge sheep farms they ran over the northern counties). Although associated with this religious order, the success of these estates led other groups to copy the practice.

The grange complex would in addition to farm buildings have a chapel for the lay brethren, although they might only number a few, with most of the work done by paid servants and hired hands. There might also have been fishponds and mills, with the whole site surrounded by a moat, perhaps even with a wall and gateway,

FIG 10.3: GREAT COXWELL BARN, OXFORDSHIRE: *This huge monastic barn with its two rows of vertical posts supporting the roof and creating aisles down either side was part of a grange belonging to Beaulieu Abbey in Hampshire. Entrance was through two porches, one on each side, with a dovecote above one and above the other a room for the grange manager. From here he could keep a sharp eye upon the corn entering and the threshed grain leaving. The door in the end wall was opened up in the 18th century.*

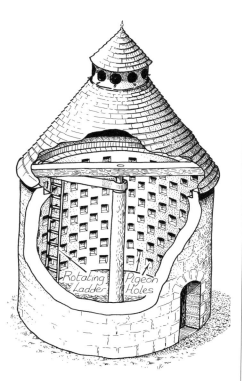

monks after blood letting or for the head of the house to holiday in, a benefit which led to such absenteeism that a royal decree had to be passed to limit an abbot to spending a maximum of three months on the abbey's estates.

Today there are fragments of buildings and numerous outlines of moats and fishponds remaining across the country from these monastic granges. A frequently found record is the name 'Grange' itself – be wary, though, many villages have a large house called a grange but these often date from the 19th century, when this was a fashionable title and may have no connection with an earlier abbey.

■ TITHE BARNS AND DOVECOTES

There are two distinctive types of farm building from these granges that can still be found intact today, the tithe barn and the dovecote. The former are incorrectly titled as they were not used for the parish tithes (one tenth of the annual produce used to support the local church and priest) but were barns where the produce from the monastic granges could be processed and stored. The huge size of some of these structures gives you an idea of the wealth that could be produced on the farms.

In the larger examples, the roof required two lines of vertical posts inside to support it, creating aisles down each side (hence they are called aisled barns). There would usually be one or two sets of doorways opposite one another, which could be opened to allow a breeze through when threshing the corn so that the useless chaff would be blown away leaving the grain and straw on the floor. Often over the doorway porches there would be a small room for the lay brother in charge of the grange, from which he could keep a sharp eye on their precious produce.

FIG 10.4: *A picture of a circular type of dovecote with a cut-away of the wall to reveal the inner recesses for the nesting birds and a ladder arrangement which rotated round the central post by which they could be reached.*

making some of the larger examples like a small monastery themselves.

From an early date, though, there were problems with maintaining a good standard of staff, and even in the 13th century abbeys were reverting to leasing out these farms, a process that accelerated in the 14th century after the effects of the Black Death upon the numbers of lay brothers. Some orders retained their granges for leisure, usually as retreats for

FIG 10.5: DIEULACRES ABBEY, LEEK, STAFFORDSHIRE: *The line of trees running across the foreground of this view marks the River Churnet, which was probably re-sited up against this side of the valley to create the open fields beyond where it used to flow. The farm building just to the right of centre in the background marks the site of the abbey.*

One of the privileges of the lord of the manor – which abbots often were – was the right to keep pigeons, and many of the dovecotes used to house them can still be found today, either on the site of a grange or within the abbey precinct. They could range from impressive freestanding structures with a square, rectangular or round plan, down to just part of a roof sectioned off, with a triangular arrangement of holes on the gable end. The inside walls were usually constructed with gaps between the stone or brick, creating recesses in which the birds lay, with ladders being used by the staff to reach them.

RIVER CHANNELS AND DRAINAGE

Abbeys appear to have been one of the main driving forces in agricultural improvement in the early medieval period, from increasing crop yields on poor land to creating huge sheep runs. One of the monks' greatest skills, though, was the management of water, which extended far beyond the supply and drainage systems within the precinct. Their work could range from the re-channelling of the rivers that ran down the valley in which the abbey stood, to the creation of banks, dykes and drainage ditches to convert huge areas of fen or coastal marsh into usable dry land. Some of the waterways they dug were large enough for boats, improving the transport of goods to these areas more than five hundred years before the canal mania of the late 18th century.

QUARRIES AND MINES

The medieval monks were also exploiting other resources from their estates, like coal, lead and iron. Their methods of extracting it were probably simple, with open pits along easily dug seams of the mineral near the surface. Stone was crucial to every abbey or priory for its own principal buildings, and the close proximity of a suitable and easily transportable supply was paramount when selecting the site of the monastery. Some were lucky and had it close at hand, as at Fountains, where the valley sides in which the abbey sits were cut out, while others made sure they were beside a navigable river, for instance, as the movement of stone by water from a great distance was preferable to hauling it along roads from a site closer at hand.

◈ VILLAGE CLEARANCES AND PLANNED SETTLEMENTS

I, along with many others, have been brought up on the pleasantly simple notion that the Saxons founded our villages and they have developed naturally over the centuries until the rapid expansion and changes of the last hundred years. As with all things in life, though, notions are rarely that simple! It is now understood that most villages took shape at a later date, some even in the 12th and 13th centuries, and that many were planned with a regular layout. It is also likely that abbeys were behind many of these schemes. Some may have been brought about by a coalescing of smaller hamlets into one large village, while others were built on new sites, perhaps on land reclaimed from marsh and fen or in upland areas associated with monastic granges. It is also known that numerous villages were destroyed or re-sited by monks, especially those of the Cistercian Order as they cleared noisy peasants out

FIG 10.6: THE GEORGE HOTEL, DORCHESTER, OXFORDSHIRE: *This ancient building had its origins as an inn established directly opposite the entrance to the abbey (it stands just beyond the gateway in the background of Fig 9.6).*

Fig 10.7: CROWLAND, LINCOLNSHIRE: *There are many other structures that are associated with medieval monasteries, such as this unique three span bridge built in the 13th century and featuring a statue probably taken from the front of Croyland Abbey. When it was built two rivers ran down the middle of the streets and met at this point, hence the three arches.*

of earshot of their new abbey precinct.

In the 12th and 13th centuries particularly it was fashionable for landowners such as abbeys to gain a charter to hold a weekly market. They could expect income from the rents and tolls for stalls and buildings that they laid out around their new market place, and if successful (as not all were) then a small settlement on the doorstep of a monastery might grow into a major town. Today we still shop in town centres that were laid out as speculative ventures by monks!

▨ HOSPITALS AND INNS

Although guest houses were built in the great courts, many abbeys also provided accommodation outside the precinct. There were numerous hospitals established to look after the sick and infirm, including almshouses, bedehouses and lazar houses (for treating lepers), and there were hospices for pilgrims and travellers. It is probably from the latter that inns were developed, a number of which still stand on the doorstep of medieval abbey sites. With the increasing number of visitors and the financial difficulties that many communities found themselves in during the 14th and 15th centuries, establishing an inn helped take the strain without stretching the resources of the community and causing too much disruption to their way of life.

SECTION
III

QUICK
REFERENCE
GUIDE

TIME CHART

This shows the dates alongside the relevant architectural period, and illustrations of parts of abbeys approximately in line with the time when the style of the feature first appeared.

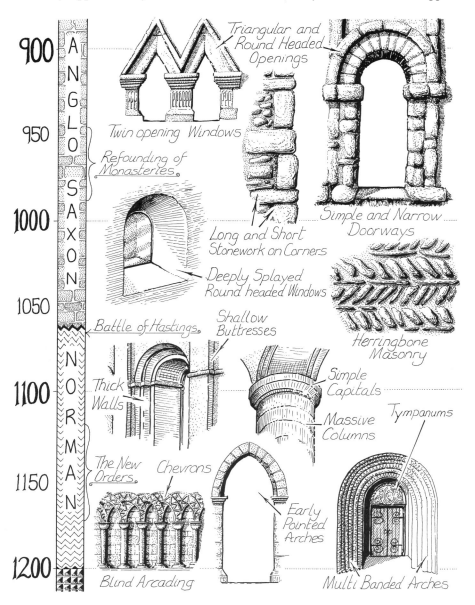

900

A N G L O S A X O N

Triangular and Round Headed Openings

Twin opening Windows

Refounding of Monasteries.

950

Simple and Narrow Doorways

1000

Long and Short Stonework on Corners

Deeply Splayed Round headed Windows

Herringbone Masonry

1050

Battle of Hastings.

Shallow Buttresses

N O R M A N

Thick Walls

Simple Capitals

1100

Massive Columns

Tympanums

The New Orders.

Chevrons

1150

Early Pointed Arches

1200

Blind Arcading

Multi Banded Arches

EARLY ENGLISH

DECORATED

PERPENDICULAR

1250

1300

1350

1400

1450

1500

1550

Lancet Windows

Composite Columns

Naturalistic Foliage

Stiff Leaf Capitals

Dog Tooth Moulding

Curvilinear Tracery

The Black Death.

Abbot's Lodgings

Gatehouses and Walls

Perpendicular Windows

New West Towers

Square Headed Windows

Fan Vaulting

The Dissolution of the Monasteries.

Flat Arched Openings

Brickwork fashionable

Abbeys & Priories to Visit

Below are listed the abbeys and priories featured in this book, along with some other notable sites, all of which are open to the public. Expect to pay an entrance fee or offer a donation at many sites (marked by *), while the remainder are free at the time of writing. The majority are in the care of English Heritage, whose annual membership subscription offers good value for money if you intend to visit a number of sites, as well as helping support their restoration work.

English Heritage (EH), Customer Services Dept, PO Box 569, Swindon, SN2 2YP. Telephone: 0870 333 1181. Web: www.english-heritage.org.uk

National Trust (NT): PO Box 39, Bromley, Kent BR1 3XL. Telephone: 0870 458 4000. Web: www.nationaltrust.org.uk

The North of England

*BYLAND ABBEY, North Yorkshire (EH): Large site dominated by the west front of the church. Notable floor tiles survive.

*CHESTER CATHEDRAL, Cheshire: A Benedictine abbey church, which became the cathedral in 1541. The cloister, refectory and gateway still survive.

*DURHAM CATHEDRAL, County Durham: This cathedral-priory is the best example of early Norman architecture in the country.

EASBY ABBEY, North Yorkshire (EH): A complete gatehouse, also good remains of the frater and dorter.

EGGLESTONE ABBEY, County Durham (EH): Good remains of this small monastery, beautifully set in a valley beside the River Tees.

*FOUNTAINS ABBEY, North Yorkshire (EH): The 'must see' abbey! The spectacular church, the Chapel of Nine Altars and the cellarer's range are located in a beautiful wooded valley. Most of the monastic complex survives in some state or other in addition to the restored mill nearby and Fountains Hall, made from stone from the abbey. A World Heritage Site.

*FURNESS ABBEY, Barrow, Cumbria (EH): Spectacular sandstone ruins set in a wooded vale with almost the complete site exposed. A 'must visit'!

*JERVAULX ABBEY, North Yorkshire: Low walls of most of the complex survive, including a large chunk of the dorter wall (pay for entry in honesty box).

KIRKSTALL ABBEY, West Yorkshire: Outstanding remains of the church and cloister buildings of this Cistercian abbey just to the north of Leeds city centre.

*LANERCOST PRIORY, Cumbria (EH): Impressive remains of the church with parts of the frater and gateway on this site close to Hadrian's Wall.

*LINDISFARNE PRIORY, Northumberland (EH): Evocative remains of the later church stand on the site first established by St Aidan in AD 635. Access limited by tides.

*MOUNT GRACE PRIORY, North Yorkshire (EH/NT): Unique example of a Carthusian monastery, with its huge cloister and rebuilt monk's cell. Later house built out of the priory guest house.

*RIEVAULX ABBEY, North Yorkshire (EH): The stunning shell of the church dominates this impressive abbey site with substantial remains of most buildings.

*ROCHE ABBEY, South Yorkshire (EH): The huge limestone walls of the church transepts dominate this clearly laid out Cistercian abbey.

ST PAUL'S MONASTERY, JARROW, Tyne and Wear (EH): Part of the church that Bede knew survives in the chancel of the present church. Nearby is the Bede's World museum.

SHAP ABBEY, Cumbria (EH): An imposing tower stands over the foundations of this small abbey a short drive from junction 39 of the M6.

THORNTON ABBEY, Humberside (EH): Spectacular gatehouse and remains of the octagonal chapter house.

TYNEMOUTH PRIORY, Tyne and Wear (EH): Spectacular remains of the church survive within the old walls of a Norman castle on a promontory near the North Pier.

*WHITBY ABBEY, North Yorkshire (EH): Evocative remains of the church dominate the clifftop setting of this abbey, which was originally founded in AD 657 and was the location of the famous Synod a few years later.

The Midlands

ABINGDON ABBEY, Oxfordshire: Remains of the checker with a unique medieval chimney and gatehouse survive from this once important Benedictine abbey.

*BUILDWAS ABBEY, Shropshire (EH): The shell of the church, a good example of early Cistercian architecture, and the chapter house are the highlights.

CROXDEN ABBEY, Staffordshire (EH): Impressive remains of the church (cut through the middle by a public road) and parts of the east range and the abbot's lodgings.

DORCHESTER ABBEY, Oxfordshire: Originally founded in AD 634, the later medieval church is still used by the parish and the guest house next to it is a museum.

*GLOUCESTER CATHEDRAL, Gloucestershire: This important Benedictine abbey church became a cathedral after the dissolution but retains not only its spectacular east window and shrine of Edward II but also its beautiful fan vaulted cloister alley.

*HAILES ABBEY, Gloucestershire (EH): A good museum complements the remains of the cloisters and the footings of the church.

*HAUGHMOND ABBEY, Shropshire (EH): The abbot's lodging and chapter house are the notable parts of this site, which is arranged around an unusual double cloister.

LILLESHALL ABBEY, Shropshire (EH): Long, simple church with parts of the cloisters, including an impressive south door and book cupboard.

*MUCH WENLOCK PRIORY, Shropshire (EH): Immaculate site with beautiful decoration in the chapter house and a unique circular laver.

*NEWSTEAD PRIORY, Nottinghamshire: Splendid western façade composed of the surviving face of the monastic church along with the house (known as Newstead Abbey) that was built out of the cloisters.

PRIORY CHURCH OF ST MARY, DEERHURST, Gloucestershire: One of the finest surviving Saxon monastic churches

*TEWKESBURY ABBEY, Gloucestershire: The impressive Norman church, with the original tower, west front and nave columns, remains in parish use.

The East of England

BINHAM PRIORY, Norfolk (EH): Norman church with a notable early tracery window in the west front (now bricked up) and remains of cloisters.

*CASTLE ACRE PRIORY, Norfolk (EH): The decorative west front and good remains of most cloister buildings survive. The prior's lodgings and recreated herb garden are also of note.

CROYLAND ABBEY, Crowland, Lincolnshire: The parish retained its part of the abbey church after the dissolution, with the ruins of the rest still standing to its side. Odd three-arched bridge nearby in the town centre.

*DENNY ABBEY, Cambridgeshire (EH): Interesting remains of the church and refectory used by three different orders and then as a farm.

LEISTON ABBEY, Suffolk (EH): Parts of the church and cloister buildings survive at this abbey, re-sited here after its earlier location in nearby marshes was abandoned in the 14th century.

*PETERBOROUGH ABBEY, Cambridgeshire: Founded in AD 656 but the later abbey church is now the cathedral. The gateway and infirmary are also of note.

ST BOTOLPH'S PRIORY, COLCHESTER, Essex (EH): The west front and the skeleton of the church, made from reused Roman bricks survive.

The South and South West

*BATTLE ABBEY, East Sussex (EH): The remains of the dormitory and gatehouse survive of this abbey founded by William the Conqueror.

*BEAULIEU ABBEY, Hampshire: The lay brothers' dorter survives, as does the frater, which was converted into a church at the dissolution. The palace was built around the monastic gatehouse.

*BUCKLAND ABBEY, Devon (NT): Most of the church survives, along with an impressive 15th century barn.

*CLEEVE ABBEY, Somerset (EH): Excellent remains of the cloister buildings and gatehouse.

*GLASTONBURY ABBEY, Somerset: The richest and largest monastery in England has only limited remains but these include the notable abbot's kitchen. Other related buildings survive in the town and surrounding area.

MALMESBURY ABBEY, Wiltshire: The nave of this early Benedictine abbey survives as a parish church with a spectacularly decorated Norman south doorway.

NETLEY ABBEY, Hampshire (EH): Good remains of the church and monastic buildings overlooking Southampton Water.

READING ABBEY, Berkshire: Ruins set in a park beside the River Kennet.

*ST ALBANS CATHEDRAL, Hertfordshire: This former abbey church has much early Norman work remaining, including the massive plain nave walls and the tower built from reused Roman bricks. Gatehouse nearby.

*WESTMINSTER ABBEY, London: An oddity – neither a cathedral nor parish church but a Royal Peculiar! As well as the famous church, much survives of the precinct and cloisters to the south, including the chapter house.

Wales and Scotland

*IONA ABBEY AND NUNNERY, off the Isle of Mull, Scotland: Restored medieval abbey buildings on the sacred site of the monastery founded by St Columba in AD 563. Notable for early Christian crosses. The attractive remains of the nunnery are nearby.

*TINTERN ABBEY, Gwent, Wales (EH): Dramatic setting in a deep wooded valley of the River Wye. The impressive church, standing almost to its original height, dominates the site.

*VALLE CRUCIS ABBEY, Clwyd, Wales (EH): Good views from the road overlooking the remains of the church and notably the monks' dorter.

GLOSSARY

ABBEY:	A monastery governed by an abbot or abbess, usually a larger establishment.
ABBOT:	Superior of an Abbey.
AISLE:	The side wings behind the rows of columns supporting the main body of the church.
ALMONRY:	The room or building from which alms were distributed.
AMBULATORY:	A passage which ran around the outside of an apse for processions.
APSE:	A semicircular or polygonal end of a building (usually the end of a presbytery).
ARCADE:	A row of columns or piers (called a blind arcade when fixed to a wall).
AUMBRY:	A wall cupboard.
BUTTRESS:	A projecting stack of masonry set at right angles to a wall in order to support it.
CAPITAL:	The head or top of a column, often decorated.
CARREL:	One of the cubicles in which monks could study, set against the windows of the cloister next to the church.
CELL:	A small building for accommodating an individual monk.
CHANTRY:	A donated altar or chapel where mass was said for the donor.
CHAPTER HOUSE:	The meeting room of a monastery.
CHARNEL HOUSE:	A building where bones were stored after the periodic clearing of graves to make room for new ones.
CHARTERHOUSE:	A Carthusian monastery (from their founding home at La Grande Chartreuse, near Grenoble).
CHECKER:	The accounts office of a monastery (as in exchequer).
CHOIR:	The part of the church between the nave and presbytery where the monks took their daily services.
CLERESTORY:	The upper row of windows in a church.
CLOISTER:	The enclosed space central to the domestic parts of the monastery, with a covered alley around the outside and the garth in the middle.

CONVERSI:	Lay brothers, usually illiterate, who performed the manual work of the community.
CORBEL:	A stone bracket set into a wall, often used to support a roof timber.
CORRODIAN:	A person who paid a monastery a set sum for accommodation in their old age.
CREDENCE:	A shelf or table near the altar where the sacraments were placed.
CRYPT:	A chamber below the floor of a church for holding a grave or holy relic.
CURIA:	The outer court of a monastery.
CURVILINEAR:	A flowing form of uninterrupted curves; usually applied to window tracery.
DAIS:	A raised platform, found in monasteries at the far end of the frater, where the superior members of the community sat.
DORTER:	The dormitory or sleeping quarters of the monks.
FARMERY:	The infirmary, where sick or infirm monks where cared for.
FRATER:	The hall where the monks took their meals, also known as the refectory.
GALILEE:	A structure built across the west end of the church where processions could form.
GARDEROBE:	A toilet.
GARTH:	The central open garden area in the middle of the cloisters.
GRANGE:	A monastic estate centred upon a storage barn and other farm buildings run by lay brothers.
GROIN:	The edge where two vaults meet.
HAMMERBEAM:	A type of roof truss where the weight is supported on a clever system of hammer posts, beams and brackets set in the side walls so that no vertical posts block the room below.
HERRINGBONE:	Stone or brick work laid in alternating diagonal layers (a zigzag).
HERMITAGE:	A cell, usually remote from a community but sometimes within a site, ranging from a cave to a complex of buildings.
HIGH MASS:	The celebration of mass with music and ceremony.
HOSPITAL:	A general term for a place where the sick, old or infirm were cared for.
HOURS:	The offices or services sung by monks at set times during the day.
IMPOST:	A moulded piece of brick or masonry set into a wall on which an arch rests.
INFIRMARY:	See Farmery.
LADY CHAPEL:	A chapel dedicated to the Virgin Mary, usually at the east end or side of the presbytery.
LANCET:	A tall, narrow window with a pointed arch, popular in the 13th century, often as a triple set.
LAVER/LAVABO:	A trough for washing in.

LOUVRE: A covered opening in the roof to let smoke out, often with angled slats.

MASS: The most common name for the Eucharist, the central act of Christian worship.

MENDICANTS: Monastic groups who lived from begging (from Latin *mendicare*, to beg).

MINSTER: A name for a monastery or its church in the Anglo-Saxon period, and afterwards applied to some cathedrals and churches.

MISERICORD: A projection on the underside of choir stalls to give support while standing during services. Also a refectory associated with the infirmary where meat was served (from Latin *misericordia*, meaning mercy). When rules relaxed in the 13th and 14th centuries the misericord could have been used from time to time by all the monks.

MONASTERY: A community of monks or nuns living under a rule and bound by vows of poverty, obedience and chastity.

MONK: A male member of a religious community.

MULLION: A vertical bar in a window.

NAVE: The western part of the church where the lay brothers or secular community had their services. Often of large size to allow for processions.

NUN: A member of a female religious community, a convent or nunnery. Nuns could not be priests so their houses relied on monks of the same order or sometimes had their own chaplain.

OBEDIENTIARIES: The officers in charge of individual departments within a monastery.

OGEE: A curved line with a concave and convex part (elongated 'S' shape).

PARLOUR: An area where monks could speak or meet outsiders (from Latin *parlare*, meaning to speak).

PENTISE: A lean-to structure or passageway.

PISCINA: A stone basin for washing communion vessels.

PRECEPTORY: A house of the Knights Templars or sometimes of the Knights Hospitallers.

PRECINCT: The area of a monastery bounded by a wall or ditch.

PRESBYTERY: The eastern end of the church where the altar stood.

PRIOR: The superior of a priory, or second in command at an abbey .

PRIORY: A monastery governed by a prior. These tended to be smaller establishments (although they could grow to be more important than some abbeys).

PULPITUM: A screen with an entrance doorway at the west end of the choir.

QUIRE: See Choir.

REFECTORY: See Frater.

REGULAR: A person living under a religious rule (as opposed to 'secular').

REREDORTER: Monastic toilet block, usually backing onto a drain or stream.

REREDOS: A screen or wall in front of which stood the altar.

RETRO-CHOIR: The space either between the east of the nave and west of the choir (between screens) where processions could rearrange themselves, or behind the altar and reredos.

ROOD: The cross or crucifix, usually mounted on top of the screen at the east end of the nave (rood screen).

RULE: The constitution laid down for the way that monks should live, and for the running of the monastery.

SACRISTY: A room used for storing sacred vessels.

SECULAR: Not concerned with church or monastic matters

SEDILIA: Seats for the senior members of the monastery during services, usually recessed into the wall of the presbytery.

SLYPE: A covered passageway leading east out of the cloister.

SQUINT: A small opening in a wall allowing a view of the altar for those who could not otherwise see it.

STALLS: Rows of wooden or stone seats.

STOUP: A basin with holy water, near to the entrance of a church.

TRACERY: The ornamental masonry pieces making patterns within the upper half of a window or blank arcade.

TRANSEPTS: The short side arms of a church, protruding out to the north and south.

TRANSOM: A horizontal bar in a window.

TRIFORIUM: A wall passage behind an arcade in a church, above the aisles and below the clerestory.

TYMPANUM: The arched area above a doorway. This was usually decorated, especially in the 12th century.

UNDERCROFT: The chamber below a large room, usually with a stone vaulted ceiling.

VAULT: An arched ceiling of stone or brick (or imitated in wood and plaster).

VESTRY: A room where vestments are stored.

VOUSSOIR: A wedge-shaped stone or brick used to form an arch.

WARMING HOUSE: A room with a fire where the monks could warm themselves in winter.

BIBLIOGRAPHY

Mick Aston *Monasteries in the Landscape*
Frank Bottomley *The Abbey Explorers Guide*
Judith Loades (Ed) *Monastic Studies: The Continuity of Tradition*
Anna Ritchie *Iona*
Michael Thompson *Cloister, Abbot and Precinct*
John L. Tomkinson *Monastic Staffordshire*
Geoffrey N. Wright *Discovering Abbeys and Priories*

General Books on History and Architecture
Lucy Archer *Architecture in Britain and Ireland: 600-1500*
Mick Aston *Interpreting the Landscape*
Fleming, Honour and Pevsner *The Penguin Dictionary of Architecture and Landscape Architecture*
Jane Hatcher *Exploring England's Heritage: Yorkshire to Humberside*
Robert Jackson *Dark Age Britain: What to see and Where*
Richard Morris *Churches in the Landscape*
Colin Platt *The Parish Churches of Medieval England*
Colin Platt *Late Medieval and Renaissance Britain*
Trevor Rowley *Norman England*
David Watkin *English Architecture*
Christopher Wilson *The Gothic Cathedral: 1130-1530*
Iain Zaczek *Ireland: Land of the Celts*

Guidebooks to the following sites:
Abingdon Abbey, Beaulieu Abbey, Dorchester Abbey, Easby Abbey, Fountains Abbey, Furness Abbey, Gloucester Cathedral, Great Coxwell Barn, Haughmond Abbey, Iona Abbey, Jervaulx Abbey, Lilleshall Abbey, Mount Grace Priory, Rufford Abbey and Wenlock Priory.

ALSO IN THIS SERIES

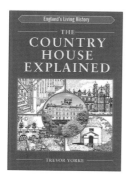

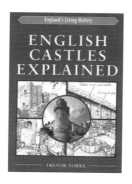

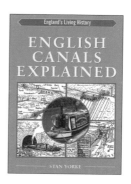

INDEX

A

Abbot: 8, 14, 15, 17, 24, 46, 52–54, 57, 59–61, 66, 68, 88–90, 105–106
Abbot's Lodging/ Halls: 53–54, 58, 70, 72, 95, 97, 98, 105–106
Abingdon: 102, 119
Alien Cells/ Priories: 25–26, 53,
Almonry: 98, 100, 102, 104
Ampleforth: 69, 72,
Augustinians: 22, 26, 30, 31, 39, 42, 44, 70

B

Bakehouse: 98–99
Bardsey: 10
Barns: 99, 110–111
Battle Abbey: 22, 49, 120
Beaulieu Abbey: 110, 120
Bede: 15
Bells: 68, 78, 79
Benedictines: 14, 16, 17, 19, 22, 24, 29, 30, 31, 38, 39, 66, 70, 78, 83, 84, 97
Binham Priory: 70, 120
Black Death: 41, 52, 54, 111
Breedon on the Hill: 18
Brewhouse: 98–99
Brixworth: 11, 19, 20
Buckland Abbey: 120
Buildwas Abbey: 29, 83, 119
Bury St Edmunds: 70
Byland Abbey: 47, 79, 82, 118

C

Canterbury: 13, 14, 16, 69
Carlisle: 69
Carmelites: 39, 42, 44
Carthusians: 53, 56, 59, 61, 86, 89, 106
Castle Acre Priory: 120
Cathedral priories: 15, 69,
Cells: 13, 14, 16, 17, 56, 59, 61, 64, 89
Cellarium/Cellar: 25, 85, 93, 96–97
Cemetery: 88, 89, 98, 103–105
Chapels: 11, 12, 16, 25, 27, 32, 51, 55, 57, 74, 80, 81, 83–84, 102, 104, 110
Chapter House: 28, 29, 34, 42, 45, 66, 84, 85, 87–88, 90, 104
Charterhouses: 56
Chertsey Abbey: 81
Chester: 65, 66, 69, 75, 118
Choir/Quire: 25, 30, 70, 74, 79–81
Church: 16, 17, 25, 27–29, 34, 39, 42–43, 45, 46, 49, 58, 60, 62, 63, 68, 70, 72, 74–84, 98, 104
Cistercians: 24, 26, 29, 30, 31, 32, 37, 39–41, 51, 54, 62, 71, 76, 78, 84, 86, 87, 88, 92, 94, 95, 97, 99, 105, 109, 110, 113,
Cleeve Abbey: 120
Cloister: 16, 25, 26, 27, 29, 32, 39, 42, 46, 49, 56, 58, 59, 61, 66, 67, 70, 75, 85–97, 98, 103, 105
Cluniacs : 22, 26, 29, 30, 34, 39, 86
Colchester: 22, 23, 120
Croxden Abbey: 37, 105, 119
Croyland/ Crowland: 62, 69, 114, 120

D

Deerhurst: 19, 119
Denny Abbey: 120
Dieulacres Abbey: 109, 112
Dissolution of the Monasteries: 61, 63, 66–68, 70, 71, 102, 107
Dominicans: 39, 42, 44
Dorchester Abbey: 103, 113, 119
Dorter/ Dormitory: 25, 37, 49, 57, 67, 79, 85, 88, 89–92, 97
Dovecotes: 98, 99, 110–112
Drains/ drainage: 26, 32, 90–92, 106–107, 112
Durham: 69, 118

E

Easby Abbey: 67, 101, 118
Egglestone Abbey: 118
Ely: 69